7 WAYS OF TEACHING THE BIBLE TO ADULTS

7 Ways of Teaching the Bible to Adults

Using Our Multiple Intelligences to Build Faith

Barbara A. Bruce

ABINGDON PRESS / Nashville

7 Ways of Teaching the Bible to Adults
Using Our Multiple Intelligences to Build Faith

Library of Congress Cataloging-in-Publication Data

Bruce, Barbara.
   7 ways of teaching the Bible to adults : using our multiple intelligences to build faith / Barbara Bruce.
     p. cm.
   Includes bibliographical references,
   ISBN 0-687-09084-9

   I. Bible—Study and teaching. 2. Christian education of adults. 3. Multiple intelligences—Religious aspects—Christianity. I. Title: Seven ways of teaching the Bible to adults. II. Title.

BS600.2.B759 2000
220'.071'5—dc21

                        00-033192

01 02 03 04 05 06 07 08 09—10 9 8 7 6 5 4 3 2

Manufactured in the United States of America

This book is dedicated to

all my adult students

who have taught me so much

about how Multiple Intelligence Training

deepens faith.

Contents

Foreword

This is the day of the adult. In education and many other facets of life, emphasis is on the adult years, those when adolescence ends and responsibilities begin, from young adult to older, older adults. We are examining the needs and interests of adults and providing many opportunities for adults to grow and change with the times.

The 1980's and 90's have been a period in which educational theorists have developed a number of schemes that pull apart and attempt to bring illumination to various theories of learning. One of the best such theorists is Howard Gardner whose ideas are the center focus of this book. It is obviously important that we Christian educators attempt to understand such theories and apply them where useful in our own field. While this is often a very important pursuit, we know that more can be made of such theories than is actually there.

This book examines and utilizes Gardner's research into the life cycle of the person with an emphasis on the adult life. When in the recent past emphasis has been on children and youth, here is the adult. We meet a new term, "multiple intelligences." Mr. Gardner uses the term "intelligences" to refer to a number of different approaches to intelligence and the activities we engage in when talking about intelligences.

Our author is anxious for us to try one or two of the so-called multiple intelligences in teaching our adult class. For instance, listing other persons in the class to assume roles of responsibility is a key factor. Thus, as teachers we do not assume that we are the only ones who can do a competent job in presenting a lesson to the class. By designating different responsibilities, we indicate our trust of the class. Through using their Verbal/Linguistic Intelligence in reading of certain portions of the material, we open that possibility. I am sometimes amused at myself when I ask someone else to read and I hear the material with their enunciation and emphasis in contrast to my own. It is of course never exactly the way I would do it, but it is often expressively done in ways that I would not.

When given drawing materials, possibly crayons with various colors, and asked to graphically portray the event in Scripture we are discussing, I am appalled by the results. Everyone's mind portrays the previous word pictures differently; and my first impulse is to say, "Oh, no, not that." But then I realize that what they mean is "that" and the class is struggling to imagine "that" through use of their Visual/Spatial Intelligence.

Another helpful approach in learning is what is called Musical/Rhythmic Intelligence. Even I, who cannot carry a tune nor read music in any way, find myself using my memory of a familiar hymn tune as I think about a particular idea. I keep wanting to say to my wife, it's like. . . . As I try to name the tune I start tapping my foot with a familiar melody, which then reminds me of what I wanted to say.

God has given us several holes in our head through which we perceive reality. Eyes, ears, noses, mouths all communicate to us when we use them. It is therefore foolish to restrict ourselves to only one or two (eyes or ears for example) that we can draw from. Since I have lost most of my sight, I find myself smelling and tasting in a variety of ways that can compensate for the lack of vision. In taking Communion, I find myself paying more attention to the taste of the bread and grape juice than I have in the past; and I am grateful for an imaginative God who provides such variety.

We can give thanks that Barbara has brought Gardner's work to our awareness and has thus broadened our lessons and daily activities.

—Dick Murray
author of
Teaching the Bible to Adults and Youth

Preface

Giacomo Puccini, creator of such classic operas as *Madama Butterfly* and *La Boheme*, became mortally ill. When he knew he was dying, he decided to create one more opera. His friends attempted to discourage him, but Puccini persisted and implored them to finish his work should he die before it was completed.

When Puccini died in 1924, Franco Alfano completed Puccini's work on *Turandot*, the final opera. When *Turandot* was first performed April 26, 1926, in Milan, Italy, Arturo Toscanini conducted. At one point the music ended abruptly. Toscanini turned to the audience and, with tears streaming down his face, said, "This is where the master died." Then he took a deep breath and continued, "And this is where his friends continued the master's work." Toscanini then turned back to the orchestra to finish the work Puccini began.

Jesus was a master teacher. He died before completing his work. It is up to us, his friends, to take his teachings and continue his work throughout our world.

In order to continue Jesus' ministry, we must *know God*. We need a personal relationship with our Creator. This book will help you know God at a deeper level. By building your relationship with God, you can share the good news with your students through your words and actions. In turn you can help them live and grow in their faith.

Howard Gardner's research in "Project Zero" at Harvard University undoubtedly demonstrates that all persons learn through at least seven "intelligences." By incorporating this research in your lessons each week, you and those you teach can come to know God through all your intelligences. You can use your most preferred intelligences and explore knowing God through your other intelligences as well.

Explore each intelligence presented in this book. Discover your preferred ways of teaching and learning. Push yourself into new discoveries about God by experiencing your less-used intelligences. Incorporate the intelligences into your lessons. Deepen your relationship with God so that you are better prepared to continue the work of Jesus, our master teacher and guide. You will be blessed to be a blessing as you equip all the saints to deepen their learning about God.

Have fun experimenting and growing!

Grace and Peace,
Barbara Bruce

Introduction

This book is designed to help teachers and leaders of adults touch their students and enable them to reach their fullest potential in learning about God and living faith.

I am an educator with a passion for working with adults. As an educator, I believe in Howard Gardner's work with Multiple Intelligences. As I travel this country leading teachers in Multiple Intelligence Training, my belief is enhanced. I observe adults draw from a well of understanding and insight that often astounds them.

This book was a hard sell. Many editors and publishers believe that adults really only want to sit around and be lectured to or discuss a topic. Some do. But most adults are eager to learn more about God and their relationship with God. This book is written for those seeking, searching, yearning adults.

Each chapter is devoted to one of the seven CORE intelligences. Each intelligence is described in detail. Suggestions are made of how to stimulate, incorporate, and transfer the intelligence. I then take adult learning a step further by providing:

* a profile of an adult who epitomizes this intelligence;
* brain research that substantiates this intelligence;
* information on setting an environment conducive to this intelligence;
* vocabulary that will trigger this intelligence;
* suggestions for praying in this intelligence;
* questions for teachers about this intelligence;
* Hebrew and Christian Testament Lesson Plans focusing on this intelligence to give an idea of how it works;
* an afterword describes several new intelligences being worked on at Harvard's Project Zero;
* tools and techniques suggested in the book.

You will discover that many of the ideas for teaching/learning fall into more than one intelligence. This is what makes Multiple Intelligences so exciting. Seldom, if ever, does an intelligence stand alone. You can build them into your lessons, because they do overlap. This overlap increases and enhances learning as it captures the best ways of "knowing" for all your students.

I am attempting to raise your consciousness of incorporating each intelligence to best reach *all* your students. You may discover you are already doing some or many of these things. This book, then is a pat on the back. You may also discover that you can easily incorporate some of the new techniques and watch your students grow in their learning and faith development.

I encourage you to make this book yours. Use it as a guide. Take the ideas suggested and give them a quarter turn to make them work for your class.

Adults are such interesting students. They are in your class because they want to be. No one is making them come. They are hungry for God's word in their lives. They know deep in their hearts that there is something more. They want a growing, meaningful relationship with their Creator.

I welcome your feedback. Let me know which suggestions in the book you are using in your class by writing to the publisher. Tell me what insights you have and what has worked well for you. This book is a living piece. It lives in your hands and through your students.

May it be so. . . .

How to Use This Book

* This book is based on brain research on how we learn and transfer learning.
* This book is designed for your whole brain.
* Each intelligence is explored in theory and practice.
* A chapter is devoted to each intelligence.
* Each intelligence is explained and explored.
* Ideas for stimulating, incorporating, and transferring each intelligence are provided.
* Prayer through each intelligence is described.
* Adult lesson plans from the Hebrew and Christian Testaments are included for each intelligence.

Feel free to mix and match the suggested activities. Some lessons seem to call out for particular intelligences. Please try to include several intelligences each session to insure that you are connecting with the most preferred ways of knowing for your adult students.

As you will discover, some activities will connect with more than one intelligence. That is fine. Layering of intelligences and activities that use more than one intelligence help to integrate the lesson.

The suggestions I have made are just that—suggestions. Feel free to take the ideas and give them a quarter turn to make them fit your specific lessons. Use your own God-given creativity and play with the ideas.

As adults discover and strengthen their creativity through these activities, feelings might surface that could be uncomfortable or embarrassing. Please introduce the "Guidelines for Comfort" (page 16) during your first session. Ask the group to read them and covenant with one another to live by them.

GUIDELINES FOR COMFORT
It is OK to pass.
Speak only for yourself.
Say only what is comfortable.
Confidentiality is respected.
Everyone's opinions are valued.
Over-participation and under-participation are equally venial sins.

Most Favored Ways of Learning

PLEASE CHECK YOUR MOST FAVORED WAYS OF LEARNING:

Do not spend time in analysis. Check only the items that you most often use when you choose to learn something.

Listening _____

Reading _____

Talking with friends _____

Studying alone __✓__

Writing something out _____

Studying to music _____

Creating a logical plan __✓__

Drawing a picture _____

Creating a map of the learning _____

Singing while I work ___

Writing a song _____

Pacing while thinking ____

Creating a rhythm _____

Telling it in
my own words __✓__

Writing it down __✓__

Creating a sequence
of events _____

7 Ways of Teaching the Bible to Adults

Seeing a video ___✓___   Experiencing it ___✓___

Manipulating objects _____   Asking "what if?" questions ___

Seeing pictures _____   Touching objects _____

Teaching something   Journaling my thoughts _____

   to someone _____   Learning the statistical

Doodling _____   reasoning _____

What patterns do you notice?

What gaps do you notice?

**This is the first step in discovering your
most preferred ways of knowing.**

An Overview of Multiple Intelligences

This brief explanation serves to provide a "big picture" of multiple intelligences.

Verbal/Linguistic

V/L Intelligence is the most widely used intelligence. Everything you do in reading, writing, speaking, or listening is using your V/L intelligence.

Logical/Mathematical

L/M Intelligence deals with cognitive skills that include but are not limited to: problem solving, creating meaning and order, linear and sequential thinking, mathematical formulas.

Visual/Spatial

V/S Intelligence is engaged in everything we see. It is perfected when we use this intelligence to connect meaning to what we observe. It also includes imaging or seeing with your inner eye.

Body/Kinesthetic

B/K Intelligence incorporates all physical movement as it relates to learning. It also means using all our senses in the learning process.

 Musical/Rhythmic

M/R Intelligence helps you to learn by incorporating sounds, rhythms, beats, tempo, and music into the learning process.

Interpersonal

Interpersonal Intelligence uses synergy and interactive energy to promote learning. It also includes the ability to "read" others and empathize.

Intrapersonal

Intrapersonal Intelligence prefers reflection and quiet time to imprint learning and make it meaningful. It also includes knowing yourself and what you need to grow and learn.

You are created with the capacity to learn in all intelligences. You have several intelligences that are your preferred ways of learning. You can expand your learning by pushing yourself and experimenting with the intelligences with which you are less comfortable. You may be pleasantly pleased with the insights and depth of learning that emerge when you are willing to risk.

Chapter 1 Verbal/Linguistic Intelligence

"IN THE BEGINNING WAS THE WORD . . ." *(John 1:1)*

God spoke the world into being with the words, "Let there be light" (Genesis 1:3). The Christian world knows God's Word through Jesus the Christ. Words, both spoken and written, have shaped and formed Christians for centuries.

The Bible as we know it began in the telling of stories around campfires. The oral tradition insured that stories of God's greatness and of the faith of God's people were passed on from generation to generation. All this took place long before there was a written word. These stories, told around campfires, sung in the psalms, and later recited in the homes of people who could not read, kept God's message alive. The words were so powerful they filled generations of illiterate but faithful people with hope.

As language developed in the written form, stories of faith were recorded to insure their preservation. Monks painstakingly copied the Bible by hand until Gutenberg's invention of the printing press made the Bible available to more people. Today the Bible and other books relating to faith help people all over the world read and know God's word.

Verbal/Linguistic Intelligence incorporates our ability to use the spoken and written word to communicate. By the use of speaking and listening, reading and writing, we explore, expand, and express our deepest thoughts and emotions. We can do this in literally hundreds of ways. For many this is the most used intelligence.

PROFILE

Connie is editor of her church's newsletter. She expresses herself well and thinks in words. She has a love of language and enjoys reading, writing, and playing with words. Connie is a good listener and often can find a story within a story to interest the congregation. She is an avid attender of the adult class and often does research beyond class time.

Careers that favor the Verbal/Linguistic Intelligence include authors, editors, poets, journalists, and talk show hosts.

BRAIN RESEARCH

Personal storytelling makes connections between past and current information. This connection helps imprint learning.

Beginning your class by discussing the last lesson helps imprint the meaning and make connections from week to week.

Ending your class by revisiting the focus of the lesson in a variety of ways helps imprint learning.

Practicing positive affirmations enhances the learning environment.

Using discussion, debate, and questions stimulates the brain to think deeper and richer.

Asking *how* and *why* questions draws out patterns that expose the limitations of thinking.

Using semantic memory by incorporating word association, similarities, and differences imprints learning.

Using acrostics helps form patterns for recall.

ENVIRONMENT

An environment conducive to the Verbal/Linguistic learner incorporates posted information, such as an agenda for the day's activities, ground rules for classroom behavior, a glossary of terms to be used or that have been used in previous lessons. This environment should be rich with written materials such as Bible dictionaries, commentaries, and other resource books. Magazines and newspapers dealing with timely issues that support your lessons are invaluable resources for this kind of learner.

VOCABULARY

Use the following words to engage your Verbal/Linguistic learners:

answer	debate	elaborate	give examples	paraphrase	recall
argue	define	embellish	interpret	present	restate
convince	discuss	explain	interview	read	summarize

STIMULATE the Verbal/Linguistic Intelligence by using these techniques in your lesson:

  * Invite your students to share a personal anecdote with a partner relating to content;

* Read or recite a poem or story that leads into the content;
* Invite students to "tell me all you know about . . ." (the content);
* Use a cartoon or comic strip related to your lesson;
* Record or ask questions that will be covered in the content.

INCORPORATE the Verbal/Linguistic Intelligence by teaching with several of these techniques:

* Read a specific Scripture verse in several different versions or translations. Compare and contrast what the writers are attempting to communicate by their choice of words;
* Use Bible dictionaries or commentaries as you study a specific Scripture passage to get a deeper understanding of the meaning of words, the cultural influences, and the traditions that undergird that passage;
* Agree to an open discussion of thoughts, reactions, feelings, insights about Scripture passages;
* Debate an issue in a formal or informal way;
* Share how a particular Scripture passage has meaning in your life;
* Study the Scripture for the sermon. Make your own discoveries and explore what the Scripture means to you to bring a broader understanding to the message each Sunday;
* Read books that offer insights and challenge understandings of Scripture;
* Write reactions to your Scripture study in the form of
    poems (see page 105 for sample formats)
    journal entries of a particular character in your study
    editorials or letters to the editor about your study
    letters to or from a major character in your study
    reports on various aspects of your lesson
* Tell "round robin" scriptural stories—one person begins with a few sentences, each succeeding person continues the story from where the last person left off;
* Record your definitions of *faith* (remind your learners there are no right or wrong answers);
* Keep a journal of miracles—share them periodically;
* Use the "jigsaw" technique—each person/small group studies part of the lesson and shares the part with the total group;
* Use "T Charts" (see page 33 for example);
* Brainstorm ideas (see "Rules for Brainstorming," page 32);

* Use a concordance—find as many scriptural references as you can for a key word in your lesson;
* Open your Bible at random. Close your eyes and point to a place on the page. Read the scriptural passage. Discover what it is saying to you today;
* Select a Scripture passage and read it each day for a week. Reflect on the message you receive each day;
* List Top Ten Reasons for . . . ;
* Read a scriptural passage. Go back and read it again, asking what participants *see, hear,* and *feel* as the words are read;
* Create a journal to record evidence of: happiness, sadness, excitement, new life, and so on;
* Read the phrase, "Christ the Lord is risen today" six times, each time emphasizing a different word to find the nuance in the phrase (**CHRIST** the Lord is risen today; Christ **THE** Lord is risen today; Christ the **LORD** is risen today; and so on);
* Create a letter that Paul may have written to *your* church if he had visited last week;
* Create a *Jerusalem Times* complete with: editorials, headlines, sports events, advertisements, weather reports, political cartoons for a unit you are studying (for example, Sarah's giving birth to Isaac, a part of the Joseph story, Christ's entry into Jerusalem, or Paul's encounter on the road to Damascus).

TRANSFER the Verbal/Linguistic Intelligence beyond your classroom by incorporating some of these suggestions:

As you discover students who prefer the Verbal/Linguistic approach to learning, you might
* involve them in doing research in other source materials;
* ask them to provide the origins of words, or ask them to lead a discussion on why one word was chosen over another in translating a biblical text;
* invite them to write a synopsis or commentary on the lesson to share with others in your class.

As you move beyond your classroom setting, you might encourage these students' participation in any of the following activities that will bring richness to their Verbal/Linguistic approach to knowing God.

Bible Study

DISCIPLE Bible Study was introduced in 1987. It is a thirty-four–week intensive overview of the Bible from Genesis to Revelation. Lives have been changed because of this commitment to study Scripture together. Participants covenant to read assigned Scripture during the week, then come together to explore their learnings. Scholars provide a video segment on the topic. Participants pray and study together as the Scripture comes alive in their faith community.

Bible study is a powerful way to learn more about our relationship with God. The Bible is our book. If we want to be faithful to it, we must find ways to study the Bible and to make discoveries about what it says to us in our lives. The Bible is a living document. Only through studying the message can we discern its meaning for us.

Check out the many and varied curriculum guides for studying the Bible. Some are short-term studies; others are longer in duration—everything from basic introductory Bible study through intensive and probing study. The important thing is to read, write, speak, and listen as you study Scripture.

Scribes who painstakingly created the first written scrolls recorded words in their dialect and understanding of the language. Bible scholars have worked and continue to work at determining the most accurate accounts of the words that were used to record our story. The focus on one word may take months of research to try to present its meaning as true to its original intent as possible. People who favor Verbal/Linguistic intelligence love to find out the meanings and derivations of words. They enjoy knowing how translations came to be. They will look up the many and varied aspects of words and how their usage can change the meaning or understanding of a scriptural passage.

Preaching the Word

Regular attendance at corporate worship to hear God's Word proclaimed for us is another powerful Verbal/Linguistic way to come to know God. Preachers and speakers spend countless hours researching and preparing to perform the awesome task of interpreting God's Word to us each week.

As the Word is presented, we need to be active participants, rather than passive listeners. We need to make the connections of Scripture to our life and our world. We need to take the words with us and to think about them as we go about our tasks of life. We can meet with others who share our love for learning through words and do a feedback session on the sermon material or talk about the Scripture for the following Sunday's sermon.

Witnessing

When we share our faith with others, we get to speak of God in our lives. We get to use the Verbal/Linguistic Intelligence by making the connections and by describing our relationship with our Creator. Each time we share our faith, it becomes stronger for us. In the telling, we relive the experience and make it more foundational in our faith development.

PRAY

This intelligence is how we pray most often. We either read a responsive prayer, read or speak the Lord's Prayer, listen to a pastoral prayer, or pray in our hearts.

In addition to these familiar ways of praying through the Verbal/Linguistic Intelligence, you might suggest these activities:

* Keep a prayer journal—where prayers and their answers are recorded daily;
* Practice a Breath Prayer—(see page 109);
* Encourage group prayer in the form of a litany with participants providing the prayer requests and the total class responding;
* Invite a "graffiti prayer" by having newsprint and markers available for participants to write their prayer requests or thanks.

QUESTIONS FOR LEADERS

* How comfortable are you with this intelligence?

* Record thoughts/feelings about the intelligence and its possibilities for your class.

* List five specific ways you might incorporate this intelligence into your teaching.

1.

2.

3.

4.

5.

* How comfortable is your group with this intelligence?

ADULT LESSON PLANS FOCUSING ON VERBAL/LINGUISTIC INTELLIGENCE

HEBREW TESTAMENT LESSON PLAN

Scripture: Psalm 23
Lesson Focus: God offers us safety and security.
Primary Intelligence: Verbal/Linguistic
Supporting Intelligences: Musical/Rhythmic, Interpersonal, Intrapersonal
   The Verbal/Linguistic Intelligence combines with the Musical/Rhythmic Intelligence as students are stimulated by listening to pastoral music that creates a mood and atmosphere for serenity. Verbal/Linguistic Intelligence flourishes as students read, listen, write, and speak.

Materials Needed: Cassette/CD tape and player, newsprint/markers or chalkboard/chalk, several translations of the Bible including the King James Version, paper and pencils for each student, several hymnals

Stimulating: Have a tape of pastoral music playing softly. Write the words "Safe and Secure" on newsprint or a chalkboard. As students enter, invite them to create a graffiti wall by writing words that come to mind when they think of "Safe and Secure." When all students have written a word or words, ask one student to read aloud the words that have been recorded. Allow a minute of silence for centering on these thoughts. *(10 minutes)*

Incorporating: Have several different translations of the Bible on hand. Make sure to include the King James Version. Invite students to locate Psalm 23 and to read it silently. Explain that this is the most beloved and well known of all the psalms. Share briefly any personal experiences with this psalm and invite students to share their experiences with it. *(10 minutes)*
   Invite students to read this psalm aloud from at least three translations, beginning with the King James Version. You might include New Revised Standard Version (NRSV), Good News (TEV), or Contemporary English Version (CEV), pausing between readings.
   Invite discussion with the group about which version they like most and least. Assure them there are no right or wrong answers.

29

Form four small groups; **OR** if some students prefer to work alone, provide that option.

Randomly assign one of these options to the groups or individuals:

1. Rewrite the psalm in a present situation (busy parent, church setting, office, shopping mall);
2. Rewrite the psalm in the negative;
3. Rewrite the psalm to a familiar hymn tune;
4. Rewrite the psalm in a form of poetry. *(20 minutes)*

Ask for a spokesperson from each group to share its creation with the total group. *(15 minutes)*

Transferring: Invite your adult students to meditate on this psalm for the week and to add their thoughts in poetry or prose to a journal.

Close by praying the psalm together

CHRISTIAN TESTAMENT LESSON PLAN

Scripture: Acts 2:14
Lesson Focus: God wants Christians to live in community.
Primary Intelligence: Verbal/Linguistic
Supporting Intelligences: Logical/Mathematical, Interpersonal, Intrapersonal

Materials Needed: A Bible for each student, newsprint/markers or chalkboard/chalk, three copies of the "Open and Closed Questions" chart (page 33)

Stimulating: As students enter, invite them to find a partner and to recall the best speech they have ever heard. Briefly share why the speech was so memorable. *(5 minutes)*
Record on newsprint or chalkboard students' answers to "What made the speech memorable?" *(5 minutes)*

Incorporating: Invite two persons to read aloud Acts 2:14-36—one to be a narrator and read the introductory phrases, another to become "Peter" and read Peter's words. Invite students to revisit the list they compiled of "What made the speech memorable?" and to compare Peter's speech to their criteria. *(10 minutes)*

Using the concept of "Open and Closed Questions" (page 33), form three equal groups. Ask each group to record as many "Open and Closed" questions as they can think of about Peter's speech. *(10 minutes)*

Invite the narrator and "Peter" to complete the reading of the text, Acts 2:37-42. Return to the "Open and Closed" questions, and ask students which ones were answered and which still need answers. *(10 minutes)*

Ask class members to read Acts 2:43-47 individually. In their small groups invite discussion as to how their faith community is similar to or different from the community described. Ask how they might go about making it more like this original community of believers. *(15 minutes)*

Transferring: Invite each student to create a list of ways for your church community to become more like the first Christian community, to begin steps to act on the list, and to report to the class.

Close with a prayer asking for God's help in becoming more like this first Christian community.

RULES FOR BRAINSTORMING

No judging (simply record the ideas with no negative or positive comments)

Strive for quantity (at least thirty ideas)

Accept all ideas (often those that appear wild and crazy can be shaped into workable ideas)

Build on other ideas (one idea will often trigger another—look for opportunities to hitchhike)

OPEN AND CLOSED QUESTIONS

OPEN (require thought/discussion)	*CLOSED (one-word answers)*
[Who do you say Jesus is?]	[Does Jesus live in your heart?]

Chapter 2 Logical/Mathematical Intelligence

"WHO DO YOU SAY THAT I AM?" *(Matthew 16:15)*

Our capacity to think and to solve problems is what sets us apart as a species. An important skill to keep adults' minds sharp and functioning at maximum capacity is our cognitive thinking ability.

How many decisions do you make in a day? How many questions do you ask or answer? Each day your Logical/Mathematical Intelligence works overtime to create a pattern of life that you choose. Consciously or unconsciously, we use our minds to filter and screen information in order to make decisions and to ask or answer questions. We establish patterns, solve problems, perform mathematical activities, understand relationships, use reason and logic.

The Logical/Mathematical Intelligence employs inductive and deductive reasoning, logical, sequential, and cognitive behaviors to perform acts of problem solving and critical thinking. It helps us categorize, interpret, and use both metaphor and technology. This intelligence attempts to find order in what otherwise would be chaos.

In our world of technology and high-speed retrieving of information, we would be lost without those persons proficient in this intelligence. However, in each of us lies the ability, moreover the need, of the mind to solve problems. We do it every day. This intelligence is highly developed in most cultures and highly regarded by educational institutions in every economically viable country. Our need to know rules, whether we need to know how many sheep we own, how much a new car costs, how long to bake a cake, or how many bytes of information our computer can handle.

One way of figuring such things out is by using reasoning skills. We take information we possess and draw a logical conclusion. On a recent trip to Israel, our guide took us to Mount Tabor. He said, "According to

Scripture, 'Jesus came into the district of Caesarea Philippi' (Matthew 16:13). We know a man could walk about ten miles per day. Matthew's Gospel continues, 'Six days later, Jesus took with him Peter and James and his brother John and led them up a high mountain, by themselves' (17:1). Mount Tabor is the highest spot in the geographical area and is about sixty miles southwest of Caesarea Philippi and the highest mountain around. It seems a logical conclusion that Mount Tabor is the Mount of Transfiguration."

Through brain research, particularly split brain research, we know that the brain is divided into right and left hemispheres connected by the corpus callosum. Each hemisphere controls specific functions. While many of the tasks of the Logical/Mathematical Intelligence fall into the province of the left brain, when combined with largely right-brained functions, we incorporate whole-brained thinking, which is greatly preferred. So, by adding creative thinking to critical thinking we can double our thinking power.

One of the ways to blend these thinking skills is to use metaphor and analogy. Jesus was a master of metaphor. Consider the parable of the sower (Matthew 13:1-9). On the surface it is a story about a farmer sowing wheat. But Jesus explains what the parable really means further on in Matthew (13:18-23), and we can get a picture of what happens to God's word. Jesus used metaphor to help people think in different ways about his message. He took God's teachings and connected these teachings with things the people understood. Jesus changed the teachings into word pictures (parables) so that the people could better understand what he was saying to them. Consider the parable of the prodigal and his brother in Luke 15 (verses 11-32), the "I *am*" statements in John's Gospel, or the Kingdom parables (as in Matthew 13:44-50). Each of these is a wonderful use of metaphor and analogy to proclaim God's word.

PROFILE

Sam has highly developed Logical/Mathematical Intelligence. He is an engineer and carries his love of logical thinking into the adult class. Sam thrives on critical thinking, discovering cause and effect, and interpreting data. He is fascinated with facts and will inquire about them if he does not find them in the lesson. Sam loves to do extra research on the Internet and brings in extra tidbits that expand group knowledge.

Careers that favor the Logical/Mathematical Intelligence include accountants, engineers, chemists, computer technologists, and most scientists.

BRAIN RESEARCH

The human brain is constantly searching for meaning and order. In the making of connections we give meaning to what we learn. For our brains to be fully engaged in the Logical/Mathematical Intelligence, we must provide "order" in the following ways:

* Print an "agenda" for each session—people need to know what comes next;
* Provide a "big picture" first so students understand where the pieces fit;
* Provide clear directions;
* Use content that provides meaning;
* Link new information to already known material;
* Make sure the questions make sense and help clarify the concepts;
* Offer intelligent choices of activities;
* Provide for sequential understanding of what happened first, second, third, and so on;
* Avoid misconceptions—make sure all students have a basic understanding of the lesson.

ENVIRONMENT

Students who prefer the Logical/Mathematical Intelligence will benefit from an agenda or outline. Once they have the "big picture" of where they are going, they can relax and fit the pieces in for themselves. They like to have a well-ordered environment and a sequential lesson plan. Things need to "fit" for them to have the deepest learning experience. They like facts and statistics to complete their learning. They enjoy maps so they can see from here to there. They like to know why, how, what, where, and when.

VOCABULARY

Use the following words to engage your Logical/Mathematical learners:

analyze	compare	determine	infer	observe	prove
calculate	contrast	differentiate	integrate	outline	rank
classify	deduce	estimate	measure	predict	translate

STIMULATE the Logical/Mathematical Intelligence by beginning your lesson with these techniques:

* Ask thinking questions related to your lesson;
* Provide a map of the area you will be discussing;
* Invite your students to "Tell me all you know about. . . ." (the content);
* Provide an outline or agenda of your lesson.

INCORPORATE the Logical/Mathematical Intelligence by teaching with several of these techniques:

* Practice using metaphorical thinking (page 48);
* Use both inductive and deductive reasoning;
* Create word puzzles;
* Discover patterns and relationships;
* Encourage research in books and on the Internet;
* Find mathematical operations in the Bible;
* Provide challenging tasks;
* Categorize facts and information;
* Use analogies;
* Create mnemonics (using formulas for remembering, A.C.T.S. for prayer—see page 39);
* Create timelines;
* Use outlines;
* Use Venn Diagrams (page 106);
* Create a Concept Map (page 108);
* Incorporate the five w's—what, when, where, why, who—of the story to make it clear;
* Incorporate "What?" "So what?" "Now what?" questions;
* Practice Problem Solving (page 110);
* Look for patterns and sequences;
* Look for cause and effect;
* Create codes to tell your story;
* Use Forced Relationships (page 48);
* Create a Pluses, Potentials, and Concerns (P.P.C.) Chart for decision making (page 45);
* Create an Acrostic (page 47);
* Check information (accurateness/clarity);
* Set up a debate over an issue using facts.

TRANSFER the Logical/Mathematical Intelligence beyond your classroom by incorporating some of these suggestions:

* Do further research;
* Conduct deductive or inductive reasoning tasks;
* Think about "what if . . ."

As you move beyond your classroom setting, you might encourage students' participation in searching the Internet, reading in books or magazines, and any other ways of gathering additional information.

PRAY in the Logical/Mathematical Intelligence by using these activities:

* Use A.C.T.S. (Adoration, Confession, Thanksgiving, Supplication) as a prayer sequence;
* Create a prayer format;
* Create an acrostic for prayer (use a word from your lesson);
* Compare the Lord's Prayer in Matthew to the version you use;
* Locate prayer in Scripture.

QUESTIONS FOR LEADERS

* How comfortable are you with this intelligence?

* Record thoughts/feelings about the intelligence and its possibilities for your students.

* List five specific ways you might incorporate this intelligence into your teaching.

1.

2.

3.

4.

5.

* How comfortable is your group with this intelligence?

ADULT LESSON PLANS FOCUSING ON LOGICAL/MATHEMATICAL INTELLIGENCE

HEBREW TESTAMENT LESSON PLAN

Scripture: Exodus 20:1-17
Lesson Focus: God gave us rules to help us live a God-centered life.
Primary Intelligence: Logical/Mathematical
Supporting Intelligences: Verbal/Linguistic, Visual/Spatial

Materials Needed: Bibles, newsprint/markers or chalkboard/chalk

Stimulating: Ask the group members to think about their day. Ask them how many "rules" (explicit—STOP at red lights or implicit—no one takes more than a five-minute shower) they followed to come to class today. Allow a few minutes to think, then ask them to come up with words to describe a world without rules. Record their thoughts on newsprint or chalkboard. *(10 minutes)*

Invite a student to look up *commandment* in a dictionary or Bible dictionary and to share the meaning with the class. *(3 minutes)*

Invite students to tell you as many of the Ten Commandments as they can. Record their answers. *(3 minutes)*

Incorporating: Ask a student to read Exodus 20:1-17 aloud to the class. Now ask another student to read Deuteronomy 5:1-21. Ask: Why do you think this information was recorded twice? *(5 minutes)*

Hand out sheets of paper, and ask students to translate the commandments in a positive framework: Thou shalt. . . . Then form groups of three to five to share their lists and create a consolidated list for their group (or in the total group if your class is small). *(15 minutes)*

Ask students to consider which set, the Thou shalt nots or their translations of the Thou shalts, they believe to be more effective and why? *(5 minutes)*

Ask: Is there cultural relevancy for today—if so why? How do you see the commandments being lived out or not lived out? What steps might you take to decide which of the commandments are relevant and which are not? *(10 minutes)*

Form small groups again. Ask the groups to compare the Ten Commandments (Exodus 20:1-17) with Mark 12:28-31 and then to discuss how living out the Great Commandment would be similar to or different from living out the Ten Commandments. *(10 minutes)*

Transferring: Encourage your students to think about each of the Ten Commandments during the next week and to decide how and why they obey or disobey it. Ask them to think what they might do differently if they were to obey all ten commandments to the letter of the law.

Close with a prayer inviting God's guidance in living out the Ten Commandments.

CHRISTIAN TESTAMENT LESSON PLAN

Scripture: Luke 10:25-37
Lesson Focus: Jesus' parable about compassion helps us to see God.
Primary Intelligence: Logical/Mathematical
Supporting Intelligences: Intrapersonal, Verbal/Linguistic, Interpersonal, Visual/Spatial

Materials Needed: Newsprint/markers (or chalkboard/chalk), Bible dictionaries, map of ancient Israel, dictionaries, Story Grid Form (page 46) for each student, paper/pencils, three copies of a P.P.C. Chart (page 45)

Stimulating: As they enter, invite students to find a partner and to discuss the following questions (written on newsprint or chalkboard): Have you ever been robbed? Do you know someone who has? Briefly describe the experience. Have you ever been a robber (if not literally, then of someone's time or dignity)? Briefly describe the experience. When have you "passed by on the other side" (avoiding a situation by turning away)? Briefly describe the experience. *(10 minutes)*

Ask someone to read the parable of the good Samaritan, Luke 10:25-37. Provide Bible dictionaries for students to look up the following words: *Samaritan, Levite, priest, purity, compassion, neighbor, parable.* Invite persons to share their discoveries. Record definitions on newsprint or chalkboard.

Ask the person to re-read the parable of the good Samaritan. Ask: Do the definitions give any insight into the meaning of the story?

Ask a person (or persons) to find the area between Jerusalem and

Jericho on a map or in a picture dictionary. Invite the sharing of insights. *(15 minutes)*

Incorporating: Make three copies of the P.P.C. Chart (page 45). Form three equal size groups. Assign the priest, Levite, and Samaritan to separate groups. Have them work to complete the P.P.C. Chart for their person. Share information and insights with the total group. *(15 minutes)*

Hand each student a copy of a Story Grid Form (page 46). Ask persons to select one character from each category and to create a modern-day story with this theme. *(5 minutes)*

Ask students to form groups of three to share their stories. *(10 minutes)*

Transferring: For the next session, ask students to create a step-by-step plan to help a neighbor.

Ask students to be aware of their thinking process and how they use it in various situations.

Close by inviting students to pray about doing something specific to help their neighbor.

PLUSES, POTENTIALS, AND CONCERNS CHART (P.P.C.)

Subject of P.P.C._____

Pluses:

1.   4.

2.   5.

3.   6.

Potentials:

1.   4.

2.   5.

3.   6.

Concerns:

1.   4.

2.   5.

3.   6.

STORY GRID FORM

Traveler	Traveling From	Traveling To	Attackers	Person 1	Person 2	Person 3
Man	Jerusalem	Jericho	Robbers	Priest	Levite	Samaritan

Sample Story Grid Form for Parable of Good Samaritan

Traveler	Traveling From	Traveling To	Attackers	Person 1	Person 2	Person 3
Man	Jerusalem	Jericho	Robbers	Priest	Levite	Samaritan
Young Man	Miami	Jacksonville	Street Gang	Lawyer	Teacher	Cab Driver
Pregnant Woman	Chicago	San Francisco	Drug Addict	Travel Agent	Doctor	Florist
Older Woman	New York	Pittsburgh	Robber	Pilot	Nurse	Teacher

ACROSTIC

Acrostic is a method of review and recall in which a word pertinent to your lesson is written vertically. Next to each letter is a word that begins with that letter and that tells about the word. For example:

C—charismatic

H—healer

R—radical

I —innovator

S —savior

T—teacher

FORCED RELATIONSHIPS

The combining of attributes of two things that are totally different. An example might be, "Think of as many ways as you can that the church is like a Swiss army knife."

METAPHOR

A metaphor is a figure of speech that implies a comparison between things that are not literally alike. The "I am" statements from John's Gospel are wonderful examples of metaphor.

Chapter 3

Visual/Spatial Intelligence

"I SAW THE SPIRIT COME DOWN LIKE A DOVE." . . . (*John 1:32, TEV*)

"A picture is worth a thousand words." This old cliche accurately and succinctly describes the Visual/Spatial Intelligence. This is the second most widely used intelligence. You literally see millions of images each day. You could not possibly retain every image of every day. Your brain records and processes these images, storing the ones it deems important. You can train your brain to hold images that are important to your learning by creating a mental picture of what you are studying. You can lock in these images in two ways: physically provide pictures, maps, slides, videos, and film clips or invite your students to form a mental picture in their mind's eye.

The Visual/Spatial Intelligence is activated in almost everything you do. From your morning routine of seeing where you are going for a shower and selecting your clothing, to reading the morning paper and recognizing the way to work, to greeting your co-workers and using the computer, to playing golf or tennis. Everything you do uses your ability to see and visualize.

The persons whose preference for learning is Visual/Spatial not only physically see, this seeing becomes an important part of how they learn. In order for learning to be concrete, they must be able to "see it." This means that you, as a teacher of adults, must provide maps, pictures, slides, videos, and so on. The CD-ROM Bible study aids are a boon for the Visual/Spatial learners. With the flip of a switch, they can actually see a town as it might have been in Jesus' time and watch as a person travels the road from Jerusalem to Jericho.

To help the Visual/Spatial student, incorporate graphic organizers.

These tools help adult students visualize the aspects of a lesson and how they connect. Graphic organizers are more than simply a display of words, they create a total image.

Using your "mind's eye" is an important part of the Visual/Spatial Intelligence. It helps to bring a story to life if you can have your adult students close their eyes and picture in their minds. Even though most of your students may have never seen the Sea of Galilee, they have all seen a lake or river. They can picture sun glinting on the water and waves gently lapping at a boat. Or in a lesson on the Lord's Supper, invite your students to image the followers of Jesus reclining around a low table. See in detail their robes, the crude wooden bowls from which they ate, the interaction of people gathered for a meal. As they hold that picture in their mind, ask them to see Jesus taking a loaf of bread and breaking it. Images such as these will help to lock the story of that night into their brains.

We know that many of the same aspects are used in mental imagery as in physically seeing. A whole science of cybernetics has evolved and studies are reported constantly of how powerfully our brains can work using imagery. World-class athletes use this technique of seeing themselves in their mind's eye performing a perfect dive or hitting a ball with precision. There are countless stories of people who have been in prison camps and mentally pictured themselves hitting a golf ball or playing an instrument. When release finally came, they were able to perform as though they had never been away. The act of "practicing" in their mind was as powerful as actually performing the task. Our brains use imagery in incredible ways.

PROFILE

Cindy is an artist and Visual/Spatial learner. She doodles as she listens. Cindy is extremely creative and sees her world in terms of pictures. She often illustrates the lesson and shares her visual adaptation at the end of the session. Cindy does much of the artwork around the church and will often be called upon to design logos or illustrate posters for sermons. (She designed the icons for this book.)

Careers that favor the Visual/Spatial Intelligence include artists, mapmakers, interior designers, photographers, movie directors, and Web page designers.

BRAIN RESEARCH

Brain research tells us that using the senses increases the depth of learning. Seeing is one of our most-used senses. Our brains convert visual stimuli to information and retention. Our brains use a visual system to locate what (the content) and where (the location) in the process of recall. We know that if people can remember a location, a specific place, and see themselves there, their ability for recall is greatly increased.

ENVIRONMENT

To create an environment conducive to the needs of the Visual/Spatial learner, begin with your classroom. Consider the walls, the arrangement of the furniture, the color scheme (or lack thereof).

A room displaying a disconnected variety of things on the walls is as disturbing as blank walls. Try to avoid overly distracting walls by removing excess clutter. Define a focal point in your room for a picture, map, poster, or special visual that will enhance your lesson. I choose a small altar. There is always a candle (visual reminder of Christ with us), a cross, and a third item that relates to the lesson. Students focus on the altar and begin to move into the lesson as soon as they enter the room.

VOCABULARY

Use the following words to engage your Visual/Spatial learners:

design	enlarge	illustrate	make	observe	reproduce
diagram	form	label	mind map	outline	show
draw	graph	list	model	represent	visualize

STIMULATE the Visual/Spatial Intelligence by having a picture or object that is relevant to your lesson in a prominent place as students enter:

* Display maps of your text;
* Display children's art work for your topic;
* Use a video clip that relates to your lesson;
* Invite students to bring in pictures;
* Display flowers or other objects on which to focus;
* Hand something to each student as he or she enters;
* Display your agenda;
* Use candles or other lighting to set a mood.

INCORPORATE the following suggestions in your lesson to help your students become more engaged in learning through the Visual/Spatial Intelligence:

* Use graphic organizers;

* Use posters/pictures;
* Create an agenda;
* Provide maps that depict the area you are studying;
* Make good use of bulletin board space;
* Use props;
* Use simple costumes;
* Use demonstrations where applicable;
* Use guided imagery;
* Use icons to indicate intelligences used;
* Write out directions;
* Use colored markers (not just black);
* Use an easel;
* Use timelines;
* Use a continuum and have students stand on it;
* Use clay or wire to create a sculpture relating to the lesson;
* Create a collage (pictures cut or torn from magazines and used to cover a page);
* Decorate your room;
* Use graphs;
* Use video clips;
* Use photography;
* Play Pictionary;
* Use puzzles.

TRANSFER the Visual/Spatial Intelligence beyond the classroom by using these techniques:

* Write or draw thoughts about the lesson;
* Locate pictures or maps to help students see what you are studying;
* Sketch their thoughts;
* Journal interesting things they see for a week;
* Encourage them to visualize.

PRAY through the Visual/Spatial Intelligence by using these activities:

* Include guided imagery in prayer;
* Find an object (candle, icon, picture) to focus on while praying;
* Look at one another as you pray;
* Look into the eyes of a picture of Jesus as you pray;

* Encourage sunset prayer—watch the spectacle God provides and pray about your day;
* Encourage sunrise prayer—watch as a new day dawns and consider the possibilities for serving God;
* Create a "sacred prayer space"; place in it your favorite things to bring you close to God.

QUESTIONS FOR LEADERS

* How comfortable are you with this intelligence?

* Record thoughts/feelings about the intelligence and its possibilities for your class.

* List five specific ways you might incorporate this intelligence into your teaching.

1.

2.

3.

4.

5.

* How comfortable is your group with this intelligence?

ADULT LESSON PLANS FOCUSING ON VISUAL/SPATIAL INTELLIGENCE

HEBREW TESTAMENT LESSON PLAN

Scripture: Genesis 37:2-11
Lesson Focus: God used Joseph's dreams to serve God's ultimate purpose.
Primary Intelligence: Visual/Spatial
Supporting Intelligence: Verbal/Linguistic

Materials Needed: Bibles, brightly colored coat/jacket/scarf, newsprint/markers for each student, long sheets of newsprint

Stimulating: Ask your students to tell you all they know about "Joseph" without any further information. Record all answers on newsprint or chalkboard. *(5 minutes)*

Ask one of your students (who has been briefed ahead of time) to enter the classroom in a brightly colored "coat" and tell a bit of the Joseph story leading up to the dreams. (Jacob married Rachel after serving her father, Laban, and being tricked into marrying her older sister, Leah. Rachel was Jacob's favorite wife but for many years was unable to have children. Finally, she had a boy child and named him Joseph. He immediately became his father's favorite.) *(5 minutes)*

Incorporating: Invite your "Joseph" to read aloud Genesis 37:5-7 slowly. Ask him to read it again; then ask: What did you see? (Allow response time.) What did you hear? (Allow response time.) What did you feel? (Allow response time.) *(10 minutes)*

Ask "Joseph" to read Genesis 37:9. Invite students to work singly or in pairs to create a visual impression of Joseph's second dream. *(10 minutes)*

Say, "Joseph went on to be an interpreter of dreams as well as a dreamer of dreams." Then tell a brief continuation of the story from the time Joseph's brothers sold him to the Egyptians, how he ended up in jail, and how his dream interpretation eventually brought him before Pharaoh.

Ask someone to read Pharaoh's dreams (Genesis 41:17-24). Invite "Joseph" to interpret these dreams by reading Genesis 41:25-32. *(5 minutes)*

Create a class mural by preparing long sheets of newsprint (local papers will gladly give away end roles of newsprint), or tape several sheets of a newsprint pad together. Invite the class members to work together to create this mural of Pharaoh's dreams. If your class is too large or some students are uncomfortable, invite some students to create a written text to go along with the mural. Display it in a hallway or lobby. *(15 minutes)*

Transferring: Invite students to take special notice of the visual world around them. Ask them to look for at least five new things on the way to work or in their home or church. Come next week prepared to discuss discoveries.

Close with prayer asking God to help us continue to dream.

CHRISTIAN TESTAMENT LESSON PLAN

Scripture: Luke 10:38-42
Lesson Focus: Using our inner eye helps us to relate to Mary and Martha.
Primary Intelligence: Visual/Spatial
Supporting Intelligence: Verbal/Linguistic

Materials Needed: Bible, two lengths of rope or yarn, this guided meditation, Venn Diagrams for each person (page 106), cinquain poetry form (page 105), paper/pens for each person, closing prayer for each person

Stimulating: As students enter have two coils of rope, one each on different tables. Coil one rope in a perfect circle; place the other rope haphazardly on the table. Invite students to observe each coil and to stand near the one that most represents their way of being organized. Invite each group of persons to discuss among themselves, for five minutes, how this sense of organization represents them. Then call time, and ask a spokesperson from each group to take three minutes to report the group's discussion to the other group. *(11 minutes)*

Incorporating: Invite your students to read about Mary and Martha in Luke 10:38-42. Then tell them you will read the story aloud and ask for their participation in a guided imagery. Explain that guided imagery is a mental journey in which you close your eyes and see the action with your inner eye. Assure them that not everyone is able to do this and that is OK. For those who cannot "see" anything, ask them to relax and listen to your voice.

Lead your class through this guided meditation on Mary and Martha, pausing at the . . . to give students time to create a mental image.

Say: "Please sit comfortably, feet flat on the floor, hands in your lap, and eyes closed. Take three deep and cleansing breaths."

Read Luke 10:38.

Say, "Become Martha. . . . See the setting. . . . Jesus has come to visit and has brought with him a group of his followers. . . . They have entered your home and are seated in the main living area. . . . Jesus is teaching them, and they are listening attentively. . . . Your sister Mary is among those listening to his words. . . . She is seated at his feet. . . . You look in from the kitchen area as you are preparing refreshments for your guests. . . . You observe the scene as your hands are full. . . . What are you feeling right now? . . ."

Read Luke 10:39. Say: "Become Mary. . . . You are seated at the feet of the master. . . . Picture Jesus as he is seated and teaching. . . . His words are touching your heart. . . . You are oblivious to everything but Jesus. . . . What are you feeling right now? . . ."

Read Luke 10:40-42. Say: "Become Martha again. . . . You are so annoyed that you speak sharply to Jesus. . . . You expect him to support you. . . . How do you respond to his words? . . . How do you feel about Mary? . . . How do you feel about yourself? . . ."

After a few seconds pause, say: "Become yourself. . . . What are your thoughts right now? . . . When you are ready, open your eyes and return to the room."

Debrief the guided meditation by asking how many of your students are Marthas and how many are Marys. Ask them to share their thoughts and feelings as they are comfortable sharing. *(20 minutes)*

Provide students with a Venn Diagram (page 106), and ask them to record "Mary" on top of one circle and "Martha" on top of the second circle. Invite them to write characteristics of each woman in her circle and characteristics they both share in the center section. Allow time for total group sharing. *(15 minutes)*

Invite your students to select a further option of one of these actions:

* Create a cinquain poem (page 105);
* Record a journal entry as Martha or Mary;
* Write a letter to a friend as one of the persons present at this gathering.

They may share their efforts if time allows and they are comfortable doing so. *(10 minutes)*

Transferring: Invite your students to create a mental image as they read Scripture.

Encourage them to use maps to locate regions and distances.

Encourage them to find pictures of life in Bible times to help frame the stories.

Watch movies or movie clips and think about how "Hollywood" creates your images.

Close with this prayer, printed out for each person:

CreatorGod,helpmetofindthetimetofocusonyou.Iknowmydaysaretoofilled withbusinessandmanythingsoflittleimportance.Helpmechoosethebetterpar tandmaketimetolistenatyourfeet;inChrist'sholy namewepray.Amen.

Chapter 4 Body/Kinesthetic Intelligence

"BUT JESUS TOOK HER BY THE HAND. . . ." *(Luke 8:54, TEV)*

Educators have long known the importance of "doing" in learning. The more you involve yourself physically in learning, the more learning takes place. Each time you engage your body through movement, manipulating objects, or employing your five senses, you are using the Body/Kinesthetic Intelligence. It is an important intelligence to maintain as you grow older.

This intelligence is one that many adults try to avoid using, while children use it naturally and easily. As we grow taller, we develop a need to "look good." We do not want to do anything that will make us look foolish or embarrass us in any way. It is safe to remain seated and to speak only when we need to. Yet, if you experiment slowly with this intelligence, you will reap benefits in the depth of learning experienced.

Brain research supports the use of the Body/Kinesthetic Intelligence by the knowledge that the more senses we use in learning something, the greater our retention. It is like saving computer information in several files; if you cannot connect through one file, you can access another to retrieve the information. If you are preparing adults for a study of the Lord's Supper, you might have them observe, taste, smell, and touch unleavened bread (pita bread) and grape juice. Tell them that bread simi-

WE LEARN	CHINESE PROVERB
15 percent of what we hear	I hear and I forget
35 percent of what we read	I see and I remember
50 percent of what we see	I do and I understand
90 percent of what we do	

lar to this was used as a staple in Jesus' time and was the kind of bread most likely to be served at a Passover meal. Invite them to take time to smell and savor the taste of this bread as they imagine Jesus and his followers gathered around the table that night.

Throughout the Bible, God and human beings act in Body/Kinesthetic ways.

* "The rib that the LORD God had taken from the man he made into a woman" (Genesis 2:22).
* "She put the skins of the kids on his hands and on the smooth part of his neck" (Genesis 27:16).
* "Remove the sandals from your feet, for the place on which you are standing is holy ground" (Exodus 3:5b).
* "David and all the house of Israel were dancing before the LORD with all their might, with songs and lyres and harps and tambourines and castanets and cymbals" (2 Samuel 6:5).
* "Then Jesus came from Galilee to John at the Jordan to be baptized by him" (Matthew 3:13).
* "Jesus took the loaves, and when he had given thanks, he distributed them to those who were seated" (John 6:11).

You use your body all day, every day. Many of your body's functions are automatic. You have no control over them. Your heart beats. Your eyes blink. You breathe. You walk and talk and eat and sleep without much thought. Because of those uncontrolled activities, you often take your body for granted. Yet, if you learn to trust your body to guide your learning, you make discoveries you can learn in no other way.

As I sit at the keyboard writing this book, my fingers perform a task I could not begin to explain. I do not think about where my fingers are hitting keys; they just do it. If I try to "think" about typing, I get confused. I strike the wrong keys. I need to let my mind go and let my body do what it knows how to do. It is the same with riding a bike, inline skating, knitting, or a host of other automatic activities. Once you master a skill, your body knows how to do it. Your body takes over. Your mind is free to attend to other tasks.

Scientists know through research into cybernetics that you do not even have to physically perform an activity to practice it. You just have to practice in your mind. World-class athletes use this mind-body training constantly. These athletes mentally perform their skill, and the body registers it as actual practice.

Brain research informs us that we must connect emotions for the most complete learning to happen. You express emotions through your body.

Sometimes emotions are voluntary; you laugh at a joyous encounter or cheer when someone has succeeded. Sometimes without thought emotions show in your body. Hearing the words to a special hymn or song can bring smiles or tears. Smelling bread or wood smoke may bring back fond memories of experiences in which you have encountered God's presence.

When you are tired, depressed, excited, or awed, people can usually read it in your body. Eighty-seven percent of communication is through "body language." Your words may say one thing; your body says something else. Phrases such as "he was hot under the collar," "her face was beet red," "she glowed with happiness" are descriptors of emotions expressed without your taking any voluntary action.

Your body provides you with signals; it tells you when you need to eat or rest. If you train yourself to listen, your body can provide warnings. The first sign of conflict is a "feeling of discomfort." Your body readies you for "flight or fight" by producing adrenaline.

The mind-body connection is no longer questioned by knowledgeable doctors. The power of the mind to heal and help the body is amazing. Numerous studies cite cures for everything from cancer to migraine headaches using biofeedback. Try some relaxation techniques after a long and busy day to experience how your body slows down and loosens up. This information from brain research is not new. For example, "Peace of mind makes the body healthy, but jealousy is like a cancer" (Proverbs 14:30, TEV). Relaxation techniques, guided imagery, aroma therapy, and a host of other tools of perceiving bring wholeness through the body.

Think of a favorite hymn or Scripture verse. Close your eyes and repeat it in your mind. Your body will react. Think of a particularly disturbing verse or hymn. How does your body react?

Develop your Body/Kinesthetic Intelligence by being conscious of your body. Use your body in the learning experience. Listen to your body as a means of receiving guidance and direction.

PROFILE

Tammy is a Body/Kinesthetic learner. She is usually the first to volunteer to be part of a drama or roleplay. Tammy is an athlete and a dancer. She is attending college and earns extra money by lifeguarding at a local sports facility. Tammy uses her body and her senses to incorporate learning most completely.

Careers that favor the Body/Kinesthetic Intelligence include dancers, athletes, coaches, actors, mechanics, craftsmen, and mimes.

BRAIN RESEARCH

We now know that movement is most commonly linked to the cerebellum, which is found behind the brain stem. While the cerebellum takes up a small percentage of the volume of the brain, a mere 10 percent, it houses more than 50 percent of the brain's neurons. We also know that movement is a key element in the learning process. This connection of mind/body is essential throughout life. We know the important benefit of physical exercise to our bodies; research now shows that physical exercise improves our ability to think, concentrate, and recall. You will increase the learning potential of your adult students by having them walk around the room or out into the hall, toss an object as a review, or tell a story. Use your body; stimulate your brain.

We also know that for optimum learning to take place we must "switch gears" every twenty minutes. This simply means that at roughly twenty minutes into the lesson, you will want to ask your students to "nudge your neighbor" and discuss the meaning of the lesson or to take a full minute of silence to reflect on what impact this information has on their life or to list at least five ways they relate to the lesson topic. The idea is to change the mode of thinking.

If it fits the lesson plan, ask students to stand and move to look at something in the room or out of doors. Take a field trip into the hallway or just a stretch break. This kind of movement will help stimulate brain power.

ENVIRONMENT

Adults are often uncomfortable with this intelligence, so you will want to develop an atmosphere of trust and acceptance. Begin to introduce this intelligence in small and nonthreatening ways. Bring in objects for students to manipulate. Introduce using senses in your lessons. Invite them to hold hands as they pray. As students become more comfortable with these experiences, you might slowly introduce roleplay, drama, simulation, dance, or body prayer.

VOCABULARY

Use the following words to engage your Body/Kinesthetic learners:

act out	build	dramatize	form	model	reconstruct
create	construct	examine	manipulate	operate	stretch
demonstrate	develop	feel	measure	present	touch

STIMULATE the Body/Kinesthetic Intelligence by using these techniques:

* Introduce items to touch, taste, or smell;
* Manipulate objects related to your lesson;
* Move students along a continuum;
* Walk around the room to look at objects;
* Invite students to move around the room as they think or talk.

INCORPORATE the Body/Kinesthetic Intelligence by teaching with these techniques:

* Play "Charades" using short familiar scriptural phrases;
* Experience Relaxation Techniques (page 72);
* Bake bread/press juice for a Communion service;
* Shape clay/pipe cleaner/wire into a faith image;
* Ask for feelings or opinions about issues in your Scripture lesson by having persons move on a continuum, with one distinct opinion at the right side of the room and the opposite opinion at the left side of the room;
* Handle coins, artifacts, clothing, water, and so on (appropriate to the lesson) as you learn the Scripture story;
* In pairs, express your understanding of or reaction to the Scripture without words;
* Roleplay a scriptural story. Then debrief as to how it felt to be each character (some examples: the good Samaritan, Luke 10:25-37; the healing of the paralytic, Mark 2:1-12);
* Invite participants to "become" one of the characters from Scripture. Ask them to put on a simple costume and to tell their version of the story (for example, the Crucifixion from the viewpoint of: Peter, Mary, a Roman Soldier, Barabbas, Simon the Cyrene);
* Experience a "body prayer"—move your body in any way you feel is appropriate as you pray. Let the feelings/sensations in your body choreograph the movement. Remember, there are no right or wrong ways to experience body prayer. Invite people to close their eyes as a way of feeling less conspicuous;
* Wash one another's feet (or hands) and talk about how it felt to serve and be served;
* Dance;
* Create motions to the Lord's Prayer, the Doxology, or any music;

* Remember your baptism. Touch water to your head, hands, and heart as you reflect on what baptism means to you;
* Reflect on what the bread and juice of Communion mean to you as you hold the elements. Meditate on the elements as you experience them with touch, smell, and taste;
* Finger paint your feelings during or in reaction to the reading of a Scripture verse.

TRANSFER the Body/Kinesthetic Intelligence beyond your classroom by incorporating some of these suggestions:

* Invite students to be aware of their senses as they pray during the week;
* Ask them to be aware of some movement they do unconsciously (like word processing) and to thank God for the physical ability to perform that movement;
* Ask students to be tuned in to how their bodies help them learn;
* Ask them to think of at least five ways they learn through their bodies.

PRAY in the Body/Kinesthetic Intelligence by using some of these activities:

* Create a personal Breath Prayer (page 109);
* Encourage people to find "sacred space" and to go there whenever they need to;
* Experience silence to hear God's still, small voice;
* Use incense or scented candles to create a mood (check first for allergic reactions);
* Practice praying with your eyes open and look at your group;
* Practice praying looking up or moving;
* Pray with head bowed toward your heart as supplication to God;
* Pray with your hands raised or palms up in an attitude of openness and acceptance.

QUESTIONS FOR LEADERS

* How comfortable are you with this intelligence?

* Record thoughts/feelings about the intelligence and its possibilities for your class.

* List five specific ways you might incorporate this intelligence into your teaching.

1.

2.

3.

4.

5.

* How comfortable is your group with this intelligence?

Suggestions for putting your group at ease with this intelligence

* Refer to "Guidelines for Comfort" (page 16);
* Some adults have difficulty with this intelligence. They want to "look good" and not "feel foolish." Encourage persons to behave in ways that are comfortable for them;
* This intelligence will become a powerful learning tool as they become accustomed to moving, manipulating, and feeling with their bodies;
* Start in small steps and/or permit them to pass if they are too uncomfortable;
* If "passing" becomes habitual, encourage them to try at least one part of the experience;
* We grow and learn by stretching our boundaries.

ADULT LESSON PLANS FOCUSING ON BODY/KINESTHETIC INTELLIGENCE

HEBREW TESTAMENT LESSON PLAN

Scripture: Ruth
Lesson Focus: Loving and having faith bring us closer to God.
Primary Intelligence: Body/Kinesthetic
Supporting Intelligence: Verbal/Linguistic

Materials Needed: Bibles, bowl of salted water, grains (barley if possible—available at bulk food or health food stores), shawl, sandal, star of David (six-pointed star)

Stimulating: As students enter invite them to form groups of two or three and talk about their geneaology. Ask them to share what they know about their parents and grandparents and how far back they can go. *(5 minutes)*

After all have arrived, ask them to walk around the room and to view all the props. Allow about three minutes to see, touch, and smell the props. Have students take seats, and ask if the props have provided clues as to the content of today's lesson. What led them to their conclusions? If they are right, congratulate them; if not, give them some clues so they can realize they will be studying the Book of Ruth. *(5–7 minutes)*

Incorporating: Ask students to form four groups of equal size (as close as possible). Assign Group One Chapter 1 of Ruth, Group Two reads Chapter 2, Group Three reads Chapter 3, and Group Four reads Chapter 4.

Invite each group to read its chapter and to select the prop or props that will help tell their part of the story. Allow time for each group to decide how group members will tell their story. Then have them tell the story in the correct sequence, using the props in appropriate ways. *(30 minutes)*

Debrief by asking your students how this wonderful story of love and faith reveals God to them. *(10 minutes)*

Transferring: Invite students to become familiar with their world in a tactile sense.

Close by giving each student a piece of grain. Invite them to hold the

69

grain, feel it, smell it, and imagine Ruth acting out of such love for her mother-in-law.

CHRISTIAN TESTAMENT LESSON PLAN

Scripture: John 8:1-11
Lesson Focus: Jesus forgives us even when the world does not.
Primary Intelligence: Body/Kinesthetic
Supporting Intelligences: Verbal/Linguistic, Visual/Spatial, Intrapersonal, Musical/Rhythmic

Materials Needed: newspaper sheets, two students to mime, Bible, paper/pencils for each person

Stimulating: As students enter provide each with two sheets of newspaper. Ask them to create a ball by crushing and forming their newspaper. Then ask the students to stand in a circle and to handle their ball appropriately as you tell them what their ball is. Begin with, "You are holding a balloon—play with it." Allow twenty seconds or so and say, "You are now holding a fresh egg—throw it in the air and catch it." After about twenty seconds say, "The egg is now a huge medicine ball, throw it in the air and catch it." Again, allow about twenty seconds. Then say, "Your ball is now a hot potato—throw it and catch it." Invite brief discussion on how it felt to do this exercise. *(5 minutes)*

Incorporating: Invite group members to remain standing in a circle. Tell them, "We will revisit our exercise as the newspaper ball becomes a stone. Put yourself into this story as members of the angry crowd around Jesus. Listen now to this story of Jesus' teaching." (By prearrangement, have two people mime the story as you read it.) Read aloud John 8:1-11 slowly, allowing the actions to be carried out. *(5 minutes)*

Invite students to sit. Debrief the experience by participating in one or more of the following exercises:
   * Journal the experience as one of the participants;
   * Write a letter to a friend as one of the participants;
   * Write a cinquain poem (page 105) that captures your feelings about the experience;
   * Write a song about the experience;
   * Create something with the newspaper "stones." *(20 minutes)*
Invite any students who feel comfortable to share what they have written or created. *(10 minutes)*

Ask students to sit and focus on their stones as they listen to your voice. Say, "Please close your eyes and take three deep, cleansing breaths; blow the air out slowly. Feel the new air entering your lungs and pushing out all the old 'stuff' that has been building up in your body. . . . Feel the weight of the stone in your hands. . . . Feel the weight of condemnation and judgment in your hands. . . . Think of the power you hold by your condemnation and judgment. . . . Focus on a person you have been condemning or judging in your mind. . . . Think of the reasons behind your condemning or judging that person—what is really behind your feelings. . . . Feel again the weight of the stone as you hear Jesus' words, 'Let anyone among you who is without sin be the first to throw a stone at her.' . . . How do you feel now? . . . What do Jesus' words, 'Neither do I condemn you. Go your way, and from now on do not sin again,' mean to you right now? . . ."

Allow a full minute of silence. Then say, "Slowly open your eyes and return to this place. Let all those who believe those words say. . . . . AMEN." *(10 minutes)*

Transferring: Invite students to take their "stones" home and to place them somewhere that is visible. Ask them to touch their stone each morning and evening and to reflect on how they have behaved in terms of judging for that day.

Close with a prayer about forgiveness and not judging.

RELAXATION TECHNIQUES

This is a method of controlling the inner workings of the body to slow down and focus:

* Invite students to sit with both feet on the floor, hands folded loosely in their laps, eyes closed. Tell them to take three deep, cleansing breaths. Encourage them to feel themselves relax. Begin your meditation at this point. OR

* Do all of the above and then say, "Tighten all the muscles in your toes. Scrunch them up tight and hold for three seconds. Release. Now tighten all the muscles in your calves—hold for three seconds. Release." Continue to work your way up the body, concentrating on one muscle group at a time. Tighten and release. When they complete tightening and releasing the muscles in their face, again invite them to take three deep, cleansing breaths. Then begin your meditation.

Chapter 5 Musical/Rhythmic Intelligence

"SING TO THE LORD, ALL THE WORLD!" . . . (*1 Chronicles 16:23, TEV*)

Most everyone enjoys music. Whether you tap your toes, whistle, sing in the shower, listen, or perform, music touches your life. From earliest times, humankind has felt the need to express feelings. In every culture there is evidence of some form of Musical/Rhythmic expression.

Music is the first intelligence to form. From infancy, you recognize the sound and patterns of speech and singing of those closest to you. Mothers' voices and lullabies are soothing and comforting to infants. Toddlers' first words are usually in patterns that they hear repeated—"Da, Da" or "Ma, Ma." What a delight to hear your preschool child sing "Jesus Loves Me," even though he or she may not understand the words. Children learn the alphabet by singing it. Many children can recognize a jingle and connect it with a specific product.

A student of mine who teaches physics told my class of how she helps her students learn formulas. She teaches the formula to a familiar tune. Students sing the formula until they know it. She told us that, on test days, you can hear almost all the students humming softly to themselves as they recall the formulas.

As we mature, music and rhythm continue to play an important role in our learning. Many of us identify hymns or songs from particular eras of our lives—my daughter immediately recalls memories of her church youth group each time she sings "Pass It On." Music triggers memories. Music also triggers feelings. Music associated with a particular event will always evoke memories of that event. A woman in a class cried softly as we sang "Let There Be Peace on Earth." I discovered later this song had been sung at her brother's funeral several years before.

Patients with Alzheimer's disease who cannot recall who came to visit yesterday often will be able to sing words to songs from their youth. Music moves us to a different time. It helps us remember and relive experiences.

Music is powerful. It can create moods. It helps learning, sets an atmosphere, develops tension (remember the music from *Jaws* that preceded the shark?). Music can calm or excite. Think of the peaceful mood that is created by woodland nature tapes or the energy created as you hear a John Philip Sousa march.

Beats and rhythms communicate. From early times communication in many cultures was through messages sent by beating drums. Beating out a message was an important aspect of tribal meetings. The joys or tensions of the meetings were often reflected in a beaten rhythm. Rhythms are the basis for dancing, whether for rituals or for enjoyment. Studying to certain rhythms is found to promote concentration and absorption of data. When the musical form of canon is played, our hearts synchronize to the beat and rhythm of that music and channels are opened to our brains. Babies (human or animal) will be comforted by the rhythm of the mother's heartbeat.

Our voices have rhythms and cadence that differentiate us. Tones and emphasis communicate as much as our words. A colleague and I demonstrate an "argument" to a college class by using only numbers (1, 2, 3—4, 5). The students know without doubt that we are arguing, although no specific words are used. My adrenaline rushes and my body reacts simply to the tone and cadence of the numbers.

All of us are capable of using music—if only to bring joy to ourselves as we sing in the shower. Persons who prefer this intelligence learn best when music is involved in their learning. Adults can incorporate a scriptural or spiritual message more readily if it is wrapped in music and/or rhythm.

PROFILE

Janice is a Musical/Rhythmic learner. She plays several instruments and loves to sing. Janice is a member of the choir and will often provide special music in worship. She leads the adult class in finding the right piece of music to fit the lesson. Janice enjoys putting the focus of the lesson to the tune of a familiar song that we can sing as a class.

Careers that favor the Musical/Rhythmic Intelligence include musicians (vocal and instrumental), composers, music teachers, and conductors.

BRAIN RESEARCH

Music is a powerful trigger for memory. Just as the illustrations I have used above are real, I am certain you have such stories of your own. Since we know this is true, think of the possibilities of using music in your classroom. Sing a song that connects with your lesson to imprint the meaning in one more mode.

ENVIRONMENT

Music can be incorporated into your environment in countless ways. The most obvious is to include music as part of your lesson. You can also use music or rhythm to relax or energize your class members. Try music as a transition piece, to change moods, or to set the stage for a new lesson.

VOCABULARY

Use the following words to engage your Musical/Rhythmic learners:

amplify	hear	interpret	perform	present	select
compose	hum	listen	play	recognize	sing
express	beat	modify	practice	represent	write about

STIMULATE the Musical/Rhythmic Intelligence by using these activities:

* Have music playing as your students enter the room;
* Invite students to write or say what the music triggers in their thoughts/feelings;
* Invite students to write a theme song title for the lesson;
* Invite students to think of a time when music marked their faith journey;
* Set the stage for the lesson by singing a song that relates to your lesson as the session begins.

INCORPORATE the Musical/Rhythmic Intelligence into your lessons by including these techniques:

* Adapt the words of your theme to a familiar hymn or song;
* Learn the books of the New Testament song;
* Listen to music: African American spirituals, Taize, praise songs, country, gospel, Christian rock. Then record faith images/feelings—thoughts/ideas;
* Sing a hymn that expresses your theme;
* Create a "rap" about your theme;

75

* Sing the Lord's Prayer;
* Listen to hymns/songs from other cultures;
* Clap the rhythm of a prayer or story;
* Sing or choral read the Magnificat (Luke 1:46-55);
* Learn the history of some favorite hymns; for example, "Amazing Grace" or "Hymn of Promise"; decide how the music translates the composer's faith;
* Invite your choir director to share insights on worship music;
* Sing your favorite hymn (take turns selecting) as a closing—explain why it is your favorite;
* Select music for your "Memorial Service" that reflects your life;
* Learn about some of the composers of music in the hymnal;
* Move to the beat of music (close eyes for those who are embarrassed);
* Provide background music;
* Illustrate a story with sound effects;
* Use nature tapes as background;
* Discover songs that have the same beat and sing them;
* Sing the Doxology to different tunes;
* Study Scripture according to the musicals *Godspell* or *Jesus Christ Super Star.*

TRANSFER the Musical/Rhythmic Intelligence beyond the classroom by incorporating some of these suggestions:

* Invite students to listen to words of hymns and to make them fit with the worship theme;
* Invite students to get into the habit of singing favorite hymns as prayers:
* Suggest that students hum their favorite hymns at stop lights or in traffic as a relaxation tool.

PRAY in the Musical/Rhythmic Intelligence by using these activities:

* Sing a favorite hymn as a prayer;
* Sing the Lord's Prayer antiphonally;
* Sing responses to a litany;
* Incorporate Taize chants;
* Create your own chants from the chorus of a favorite hymn;
* Clap to the rhythm of praise songs;
* Create a "rap" prayer.

QUESTIONS FOR LEADERS

* How comfortable are you with this intelligence?

* Record thoughts/feelings about the intelligence and its possibilities for your class.

* List five specific ways you might incorporate this intelligence into your teaching.

1.

2.

3.

4.

5.

* How comfortable is your group with this intelligence?

ADULT LESSON PLANS FOCUSING ON MUSICAL/RHYTHMIC INTELLIGENCE

HEBREW TESTAMENT LESSON PLAN

Scriptures: Psalms 8; 27; 51; 70; 100
Lesson Focus: The psalms tell faith stories.
Primary Intelligence: Musical/Rhythmic
Supporting Intelligences: Verbal/Linguistic, Visual/Spatial

Materials Needed: Tape/CD player and tape/CD of praise music or familiar hymns.

Stimulating: As students enter the room play a CD or tape of praise music or familiar hymns.

Form groups of two or three students, depending on class size. Ask students to name a hymn that speaks to their faith and explain why. Bring the total group together and invite sharing as people are comfortable. *(10 minutes)*

Incorporating: Record each of these Psalms—8; 27; 51; 70; 100—on a separate sheet of newsprint.

Explain that the psalms are the "hymns" of the Hebrew Testament. Many of them are believed to have been written by David. Form five small groups; or if your class is small, form at least two groups. Assign the psalms accordingly. Invite groups to read their psalm in Scripture. Ask them to select one or more of the following activities to do with their psalm:

* Illustrate it;
* Sing/chant/rap it;
* Write a short story or poem about what it says to you.

Allow fifteen minutes for groups to work on their psalm. Then bring the total group together to share what each small group has done with its psalm. *(30 minutes)*

Read Psalm 23 in several different versions of the Bible (NRSV, TEV, KJV, CEV). Discuss similarities and differences in the text. *(10 minutes)*

79

Transferring: Invite students to pay more attention to the words or melodies of music that touch their hearts and then reflect on the reasons.

Close with reading or by reciting Psalm 23 (King James Version if possible), and allow for a full minute of silent meditation.

CHRISTIAN TESTAMENT LESSON PLAN

Scripture: Luke 1:46-55
Lesson Focus: Mary's faith is a key point in the Christmas story.
Primary Intelligence: Musical/Rhythmic
Supporting Intelligence: Verbal/Linguistic

Materials Needed: Tape/CD player and tape/CD of Christmas music, Bibles, a hymnal for each person, two sheets of newsprint/markers or chalkboard/chalk with the words "ADVENT" and "CHRISTMAS" printed on them

Stimulating: Have Advent (or Christmas) music playing as students enter.

Ask students to look through the hymnal and to discover which songs might be Advent songs and which are Christmas songs and why. Invite them to record their answers on newsprint or chalkboard under "ADVENT" or "CHRISTMAS." Ask them to continue by discussing their feelings about singing Christmas songs during the Advent Season. Bring the total group together for a brief synopsis of their discussion. *(25 minutes)*

Incorporating: Tell the story of the Annunciation from Luke 1:26-45 in your own words, or invite one of your students to read it from the Bible. Ask the group to imagine what that young woman, probably a teenager, might have been thinking or feeling. Allow time for brief discussion. *(10 minutes)*

Ask them to read the Magnificat from Luke 1:46-55. Have several versions of the Bible available so students can read it in more than one translation. Ask students to discuss the differences in wording, and ask them to rewrite the Magnificat in their own words. *(20 minutes)*

Transferring: Invite students to focus on the music that tells the story of both Advent and Christmas and how important that music is to our understanding of the birth narrative.

Close by asking them to find as many songs as they can in the hymnal that deal with Mary. Sing the first verse of as many as you have time for.

Chapter 6 Interpersonal Intelligence

"TWO ARE BETTER OFF THAN ONE, BECAUSE TOGETHER THEY CAN WORK MORE EFFECTIVELY." ... (*Ecclesiastes 4:9, TEV*)

Interpersonal Intelligence revolves around a synergistic process in which the whole is greater than the sum of the parts—or—together, we are better than any one individually. This intelligence uses the understanding of interactions among people and how these interactions work to help us learn.

Interpersonal Intelligence is the most complex of all the intelligences, including many cognitive skills such as: observation, verbal and nonverbal communication, team building, understanding conflict and using it as an opportunity to grow, learning to trust, respect for diversity, listening, negotiating, compromising, and building on ideas. Also important in this intelligence are the less cognitive, but equally important, factors including: caring about others' feelings, motivation, sympathy, empathy, and a desire to work as a group for the common good.

We live in an interconnected world. By design or default, we can seldom work in isolation to produce a final product. Rather, each of us contributes our skills, expertise, or questions to create an end product that is better—due to cooperative effort—than any of us could produce alone.

We are seldom taught these skills for interpersonal learning, yet they contribute greatly to nearly every aspect of our lives. We can promote these skills and encourage students of every age to work together, to build on one another's views, and to learn from the wisdom of others.

Establishing and adhering to Guidelines for Comfort is an important part of interpersonal learning (page 16). When the class first comes together (or together again), focus on the guidelines and discuss why they are important. Group ownership and a covenant to adhere to the guidelines is a vital step in setting the climate for interpersonal learning. Refer to the guidelines frequently, and make additions or corrections as the group feels the need.

Paul's first letter to the people at Corinth provides a wonderful metaphor for interpersonal or synergistic behavior. In Chapter 12, verses 12-31, Paul uses the image of one body (of Christ) and how each part works for the good of the whole. Just like different members of the body, in interpersonal learning, we work together, using our God-given gifts to create a special community for the betterment of the whole people of God.

In Bible study we can read, do research, and reflect on our own (Intrapersonal learning); but many people learn best in community—when we share information, insights, experiences, and our own perspective.

Likewise, we can pray alone; but there is an unexplainable power in corporate prayer that creates a feeling of unity and purpose. To hear several hundred voices reciting the Twenty-third Psalm or singing the "Hallelujah Chorus" is a unique and unparalleled experience.

When we join our gifts, our diversity, our uniqueness for a common purpose of learning about God and God's interaction with God's people, we grow in powerful and profound ways.

PROFILE
Sarah is an interpersonal learner. She is a retired school teacher and learns best when she is fully engaged in discussion and analysis of the lesson. Sarah is the one who most often will lead the discussion and urge her group to delve deeper into the subject. She encourages people to talk without intimidation or stress.

Remember that everything we do is affected by our interpersonal intelligence. However, people who lead from their interpersonal intelligence tend to find careers that include talk show hosts, reporters, teachers, trainers, or salespersons.

BRAIN RESEARCH
We now know that cooperative learning is compatible with the functioning of the brain. Teachers who use only one-sided information sharing (lecture) are doing their students a disservice.

We are coming to learn more about the importance of sharing our stories through socialization. Essentially, we are social beings. We learn as we listen to others and as we share our own story.

We learn best when we connect new information to what we already know. One of the most powerful ways to do this is to compare similar experiences and to make the connections ourselves. For centuries, providing mentors or establishing apprenticeships has been a fulfilling way to learn.

ENVIRONMENT

To create an environment conducive to the interpersonal learner, provide opportunity for small-group or one-on-one discussion. Give time to share thoughts and feelings about what is going on in the lesson and how it connects with personal lives. Encourage group projects within and beyond the class session.

VOCABULARY

Use these words to engage your Interpersonal learners:

associate	decide	encounter	interview	present	show
brainstorm	discuss	explain	motivate	roleplay	teach
coach	empathize	give feedback	organize	share	translate

STIMULATE the Interpersonal Intelligence by using these techniques in your session:

* Have questions posted. As students enter invite them to pair up and discuss the questions;
* Set students up in two rows facing one another. Ask a question and invite partners to share answers. Then ask one row to "rotate" so they answer the next question with a new partner;
* Encourage small-group work and discussion throughout the lesson.

INCORPORATE the Interpersonal Intelligence by teaching with several of these techniques:

* Create your own "Guidelines for Comfort";
* As a group, decide what happens when the guidelines are abused;
* When someone abuses a guideline, use the class-devised method to make him or her aware of the abuse—and talk about how it feels;
* Share your week in groups of two or three;
* Establish prayer partners;
* Form a small group, and assign each person to research a part of the story—tell the story as a group;

* Celebrate one another's joys, and support one another in sorrows;
* In small groups work together to tell the story through

a picture	a map
a song	a drama
a mobile	a game
a comic strip	a poem
a newspaper	a rap

* Practice telling the story with two people—A and B. A begins the story and gives three or four lines, B picks up the story for three or four lines, A and B continue until the story is completed;
* Use the above procedure with three or four people;
* Each one teach one: each person learns about a particular Bible character and teaches someone else about the character. Continue this practice until each person has learned from the others;
* Create a "jigsaw" story with each person contributing a part;
* Create a Venn Diagram (page 106) with another person about the story;
* Create a group Concept Map (page 108) of the story with a partner;
* Come to group consensus on the message of the story—be aware of your process;
* Hold a debate, with each team working together to plan strategy;
* Reflect on Scripture together—practice listening and acceptance.

TRANSFER the Interpersonal Intelligence beyond your classroom by incorporating one of these suggestions:

* Invite groups to share how they may work together at home or at work to get a job done;
* Ask the group to list advantages and disadvantages of working together.
* Ask persons to record their experiences at home or at work when they have benefited from being able to "read" another person or to practice empathy.

PRAY in the Interpersonal Intelligence by using these activities:

* Incorporate prayer partners, in which two people meet regularly for a period of time and share their prayer needs with each other and then agree to pray for each other;
* Share joys and concerns as a total group and pray together;
* Create litanies and ask for personal input.

QUESTIONS FOR LEADERS

* How comfortable are you with this intelligence?

* Record thoughts/feelings about the intelligence and its possibilities for your class.

* List five specific ways you might incorporate this intelligence into your teaching.

1.

2.

3.

4.

5.

* How comfortable is your group with this intelligence?

ADULT LESSON PLANS FOCUSING ON INTERPERSONAL INTELLIGENCE

HEBREW TESTAMENT LESSON PLAN

Scripture: Job 1; 2; 3; 4; 8; 11; 31; 38
Lesson Focus: How do we react when tragedy strikes?
Primary Intelligence: Interpersonal
Supporting Intelligences: Verbal/Linguistic, Intrapersonal

Materials Needed: Bibles for everyone, newsprint and markers as needed.

Stimulating: As students enter ask them to form small groups of three or four and discuss a time when something tragic happened to them or someone they know. Ask them to discuss briefly how this person reacted to the tragedy. Allow a brief total group sharing.

Then ask the group to tell you everything they know about Job. Record the answers on newsprint or chalkboard without comment. *(15 minutes)*

Incorporating: Form four equal-sized groups (even if it is only two per group, or double up if your class is small). Explain that they will be working together in small groups in what is called jigsawing or chunking. Each group will be assigned part of the story of Job. The group will read and present its part of the story as part of the whole to the total group. Each group will only be responsible for its part. Assign Group One Chapters 3 and 31 (Job), Group Two Job 4 (Eliphaz), Group Three Job 8 (Bildad), and Group Four Job 11 (Zophar). Tell them they will have fifteen minutes to read their chapter and to synthesize it as a group to get a feeling for their person. Then they may choose to present their person as a group or choose one person from their group to present their person in the drama. Tell them they must empathize and react to the other players as the drama unfolds. You (or select one person) will be the narrator and tell the story of Job from Chapters 1 and 2. After the introduction, group members will interact with other members of the class as they present their dramatic interpretation of the story of Job. After an appropriate length of time, ask the narrator to close by reading Chapter 38. *(30 minutes)*

Ask them to return to their small groups and to respond to God's answer to Job as they believe their person would. Allow a brief sharing time with the total group. *(10 minutes)*

Transferring: Ask group members to close their eyes and reflect on this story and how it affects them personally. *(5 minutes)*

Close with a prayer for responding with acceptance and faith to what life has in store for us.

CHRISTIAN TESTAMENT LESSON PLAN

Scripture: Matthew 4:18-20
Lesson Focus: Working together and sharing our faith
Primary Intelligence: Interpersonal
Supporting Intelligences: Logical/Mathematical, Intrapersonal, Verbal/Linguistic

Materials Needed: Copies of "Biblical Brainbuster" (page 89), copies of "Top 6 Reasons to Follow Jesus" (page 90), pencils, newsprint, markers

Stimulating: As students enter give each group of three a copy of the "Biblical Brainbuster." Tell them they have five minutes to solve the BBB as a team. At the end of five minutes, invite groups to present their answers. (See page 112 for answers.) Ask: How did the experience of working together feel? Allow for total group discussion. *(10 minutes)*

Incorporating: Read Matthew 4:18-20 aloud. Invite class members to form different groups of three. Give each group one sheet of newsprint and a marker. Give each student a copy of "Top 6 Reasons to Follow Jesus" (page 90). Ask them to fill out this paper individually. Then form their group of three, come to a consensus, and create a group "Top 6 Reasons to Follow Jesus." Tell them they will have twenty minutes to work together to complete this task. They will need to share their list, listen to the two other lists in their group, decide how they will make the decision for the group list, and then create their composite list on newsprint. At the end of twenty minutes, ask if more time is needed. Give another two to three minutes if it is required. *(30–33 minutes)*

Ask groups to share their lists. When all have shared their lists, ask for a debrief of the processes they used to come to consensus. *(10 minutes)*

Transferring: Ask: How does your experience today relate to functioning as a Christian beyond the classroom? *(10 minutes)*

Close with a prayer for help in working together, listening, really hearing, being patient and willing to solve problems and to create harmony in any relationship.

BIBLICAL BRAINBUSTER

Each line contains words and numbers that will complete a statement from the Bible. Look at the example and have fun.

EXAMPLE: 40 D_____ and N_____ of the G_____ F_____

40 D(days) and N (nights) of the G(Great)   F(Flood)

66 B_____ in the B_____

12 T_____ of I_____

40 Y_____M_____ was L_____

12 D_____ of J_____

10 C_____ G_____ gave to M_____

16 C_____ in the G_____ of M _____

7 D_____ G_____ C_____ the W_____

3 D_____J_____ was in the B_____ of a F_____

4 H_____ of the A_____

30 P_____ of S_____ J_____ was P_____

TOP 6 REASONS TO FOLLOW JESUS

1. _____

2. _____

3. _____

4. _____

5. _____

6. _____

Chapter 7 Intrapersonal Intelligence

"AFTER HE HAD DISMISSED THE CROWDS, [JESUS] WENT UP THE MOUNTAIN BY HIMSELF TO PRAY." . . . (*Matthew 14:23*)

This is the second of two of the "personal" intelligences: *Intrapersonal*, which deals essentially with a person's ability to gaze inward, to examine and understand his/her own feelings and *Interpersonal*, which looks outward to deal with the feelings and behaviors of others.

Being alone or quiet to have time to reflect is an indication of intrapersonal intelligence. Often teachers and leaders are intent on covering certain "concepts" or "information" in a given period of time. The clock is your enemy; you feel you must cover so much before the time elapses, so you keep up the pace of the lesson. Slow down and allow persons time to be quiet and listen for God's still, small voice.

Time to reflect and to respond out of that reflection can produce powerful insights into God's presence in one's life and God's interaction with God's people throughout the ages, even today. When we neglect this quiet, personal, processing time, much of the lesson is never imprinted; and learning is shallow, with little meaning.

Your intrapersonal intelligence can lead you on a deep inward journey where you can take responsibility for your learning by making choices and decisions. You can set your own goals for learning and create a plan to achieve those goals.

PROFILE

Carl is an intrapersonal learner. He is most often quiet and reflective; but when he does offer an opinion, it is usually well thought out and insightful. Carl needs time to reflect and think. He enjoys being in a small group and likes to listen to others while he is forming his own opinions. Carl does not feel threatened or pressured by the group to respond.

The personal intelligences are present in all careers. How we deal with our chosen profession is determined by our personal approach to it. Those who favor the Intrapersonal Intelligence will find time to think and reflect on whatever they choose to do.

BRAIN RESEARCH

We know that time for reflection is critical for meaningful learning to take place. Since we know that meaning is generated from within, not allowing reflection time defeats the teacher's purpose. We need time to process new learning and ways of connecting it with what we already know. Adults come with a richness of life experience. A wonderful way to create new learning is to allow time and hooks to make connections. I often call this "incubation" time. The brain recycles information and that may be when the most important learning takes place.

ENVIRONMENT

To have an environment conducive to the Intrapersonal Intelligence, you, as leader, must be a role model and be intentional about incorporating this intelligence. You must allow for (insist on) quiet time—for the spiritual quality of listening for God's still, small voice. Or, request a minute of silence for reflective thought before allowing answers. You might provide next week's Scripture so that those who prefer the Intrapersonal Intelligence will have time to read and reflect on it at home.

A break for a minute each fifteen to twenty minutes may be helpful, or use quiet time as a transition between activities.

VOCABULARY

Use these words to engage your Intrapersonal learners:

analyze	conclude	discriminate	interpret	reflect	track
assimilate	decide	explore	plan	select	validate
concentrate	defend	focus	prepare	think	write

STIMULATE Intrapersonal Intelligence by

* Allowing a time of transition from outside to inside the classroom;
* Using quiet music in the background as a settling, soothing technique;
* Incorporating a beginning or ending ritual of thirty seconds of silent prayer;

* Allowing time to reflect on the Scripture for the day;
* Allowing persons to connect with their feelings in a private way.

INCORPORATE Intrapersonal Intelligence by using these techniques.

* Eliminate as much stress as possible by abiding by your "Guidelines for Comfort" (see page 16);
* Allow "wait time" for answers to questions (ten seconds will do);
* Encourage journaling;
* Write letters to or from a person in your study;
* Create a mind journey to the time of your study—allow time for visualization;
* Read a Scripture verse and ask persons what they see, hear, feel;
* Ask questions such as
    what do you think he or she was feeling?
    how might you react in this situation?
    what are some possible alternatives?
* Invite students to set their learning goals;
* Encourage independent study;
* Practice focusing/concentrating time;
* Practice problem solving;
* Ask what if? and why?

TRANSFER Intrapersonal Intelligence beyond your classroom by incorporating one of these suggestions:

* Model using quiet, reflective time;
* Suggest your students use reflection time while walking, at stop lights, or in check out lines.

PRAY in Intrapersonal Intelligence, often the most widely practiced, by suggesting these techniques:

* Encourage people to pray silently and in private, making their prayers personal conversations with God;
* Allow for a "minute" of silent prayer during a worship service, since people are not always comfortable speaking aloud in a group setting;
* Set aside a silent time for individuals to lift up to God things that lay heavy on their hearts;
* Encourage students to keep prayer journals.

QUESTIONS FOR LEADERS

* How comfortable are you with this intelligence?

* Record thoughts/feelings about the intelligence and its possibilities for your class.

* List five specific ways you might incorporate this intelligence into your teaching.

1.

2.

3.

4.

5.

* How comfortable is your group with this intelligence?

ADULT LESSON PLANS FOCUSING ON INTRAPERSONAL INTELLIGENCE

HEBREW TESTAMENT LESSON PLAN

Scripture: Isaiah 11:1-10
Lesson Focus: Isaiah's vision of a peaceable kingdom
Primary Intelligence: Intrapersonal
Supporting Intelligences: Verbal/Linguistic, Visual/Spatial, Musical/Rhythmic

Materials Needed: Bibles, candle, tape/CD of peaceful music, tape/CD player, newsprint/markers or chalkboard/chalk, paper and pencils for each student

Stimulating: As students enter have peaceful music playing softly and a lit candle in the center of the room.

Invite students to sit quietly and reflect on what the word *peaceful* means to them. Then ask students who wish to record their thoughts on a "graffiti chart" on the wall. *(5 minutes)*

Incorporating: Invite someone to read Isaiah 11:1-10 aloud. Then ask class members to relax, close their eyes, and create a picture in their minds of what this Scripture might look like to them. Ask the reader to re-read the Scripture slowly, allowing time for students to focus and concentrate on the images. *(10 minutes)*

Invite students to select a method of reporting what they saw and heard by offering these choices:

1. Write a journal entry describing what you saw, heard, and felt concerning the Scripture.

2. Draw a mural alone or with others to capture the feeling of the peaceable kingdom.

3. Discuss your thoughts about this Scripture with one or two others.

4. Write a prayer, poem, or song that reflects your feelings on this Scripture.

Allow fifteen minutes for these activities. Then invite those who wish to share their creation with the total group. *(20 minutes)*

Transferring: Invite students to think about what they may do individually or collectively to bring about any part of Isaiah's vision. They may use this vision as a metaphor or be literal. After allowing time to silently reflect on how they might bring about this vision, invite them to return to one of the activities from the previous exercise and journal; draw; discuss; or write a prayer, poem, or song about their feelings. Invite students to be aware of quiet time for the following week and to journal where and when they have made time to listen for God and what the results were. *(20 minutes)*

Close by inviting silent prayer asking God to help you be an instrument to bring about the peaceable kingdom in your world.

CHRISTIAN TESTAMENT LESSON PLAN

Scripture: Matthew 16:13-19
Lesson Focus: Who and Whose we are
Primary Intelligence: Intrapersonal
Supporting Intelligences: Logical/Mathematical, Verbal/Linguistic

Materials Needed: paper, pencils, "I Am Statements of Jesus" from John's Gospel (page 107)

Stimulating: As students enter provide them with the "Personal 'I Am' Statements" sheet (page 107). Invite them to complete the statement "I am" as a personal reflection for each of the statement stems. *(5 minutes)*

Ask: Was this an easy or difficult task? Why? *(5 minutes)*

Then ask students to read each of the metaphorical statements from John's Gospel ("The 'I Am' Statements of Jesus," page 107), reflect on them, and decide which of the statements speaks most personally to them. *(10 minutes)*

Incorporating: Invite your students to take everything out of their laps, sit comfortably, and close their eyes. Read Matthew 16:13-15. Ask your students to answer this question, "But who do you say that I am?" in their own minds. After a full minute of silence, read verses 15-19 of Matthew 16. Invite students to respond to the statement, "You are Peter [*Petros* means "rock" in Greek], and on this rock I will build my church," in one or more of the following ways:

> journal your thoughts;
> write a note to a friend who does not know Jesus;
> respond as Peter might have to that statement;

> create a cinquain poem (page 105);
> write words to a familiar tune;
> draw a picture.

(15–20 minutes)

When time is up, assure them it is not necessary, but ask if anyone would like to share what he or she has written or created. *(10 minutes)*

Transferring: Encourage your students to take time to think during each day about who and Whose they are.

Close with a prayer asking God to help you know at a deeper level who and Whose you are.

Afterword

As an educator and a Christian educator, I believe in Multiple Intelligences (MI) with all my heart. Having said that unequivocally, let me share my thoughts on where MI fits into adult Christian education.

Most educators today agree that "the way we've always done it" is no longer effective in reaching everyone's greatest learning potential. Educators across the board no longer believe that all people learn in the same ways or that instruments that test only Verbal/Linguistic and Logical/Mathematical intellect are totally valid in determining a person's "intelligence."

Beyond this point there is much disagreement. Howard Gardner states in his latest book, *Intelligence Reframed* (Basic Books, 1999; page 89): "MI theory is in no way an educational prescription. . . . Educators are in the best position to determine whether and to what extent MI theory should guide their practice." This is good advice and what I have taught all along. Use what works best for your class in your church to bring adults closer to God.

The question I get asked most in training events is, "Am I supposed to use every intelligence in every lesson?" The answer is, "No." To attempt that type of teaching would be to set up artificial rules and force-fit a theory in where it does not belong.

My intent is to
* raise consciousness about many ways of knowing;
* to give permission to try new approaches with adults;
* to tap into resources and insights that will broaden faith;
* to guide adult students in using their most preferred ways of knowing to deepen their relationship with God.

Gardner talks in his latest book about the possibility of adding new intelligences. On page 47 of *Intelligence Reframed* he states: "Here, I consider directly the evidence for three 'new' candidate intelligences: a *naturalist intelligence*, a *spiritual intelligence*, and an *existential intelligence*. The strength of the evidence for these varies, and whether or not to declare a certain human capacity another type of intelligence is certainly a judgment call." I have made my own judgment call and decided not to include them in this book for the following reasons:

1. I have attempted to work with the Naturalist Intelligence; and while I can see it evidenced in some folks, I humbly believe it is simply a deep appreciation of nature. These folks find meaning and messages in the natural world. I do not, however, believe it has the same breadth and depth as the seven CORE intelligences.

2. I believe we, as Christians, view Existential and Spiritual realms in a different light than the secular world does. For believers, there is no question of a spiritual realm; but it has nothing to do with mysticism or cosmic entities. For us it has to do with a faith in and relationship with our God. Additionally, to attempt to define a spiritual truth that is available only to a certain few who follow a specific path smacks of dogma rather than faith.

3. I believe that you can work with the seven CORE intelligences to help your adult students come to "know" God. By encouraging them to work through their own insights and discoveries, you will be blessed to be a blessing.

4. I believe that there is additional research to be done.

5. I believe that our attempts to help people understand how they are fearfully and wonderfully made will provide tools to reach all who want to know God at a deep and personal level.

There is excited stirring among educators about emotional inelligence. Emotions kick in before we have time to process or think about our reactions. We need to be aware of and acknowledge our emotions as part of who we are as adults. Through my research of the brain and learning, I have come to believe strongly in the emotional aspect of learning. I believe that emotions are attached to all intelligences; and, in fact, learning does not happen in the absence of emotions.

In conclusion, I believe that a future without MI is doing a disservice to the process of teaching/learning. You must find ways to reach your students that help them make their own discoveries. Multiple Intelligence Theory provides the way and the means to tap into the preferred intelligences of all your students. Learning takes on new meaning. Learning becomes exciting and challenging.

I further believe there is more to be discovered about the way people learn. There is always something new to challenge and inform about the exciting process of teaching/learning. By allowing yourself to break out of old patterns and beliefs, you can better equip the saints for their ministry of living God's way.

Appendix

If Your Students' Preference for Learning is . . .

Verbal/Linguistic: **Reading, Writing, Speaking**
Include:

creative writing	poetry	debate	storytelling
jokes/limericks	vocabulary	journaling	discussion

Logical/Mathematical: **Problem solving, Sequencing, Ordering**
Include:

abstract symbols	outlining	numbers sequence	syllogisms
pattern discernment	calculations	deciphering codes	cataloging

Visual/Spatial: **Looking at charts, pictures, objects; Drawing**
Include:

guided imagery	mind mapping	costumes	sculpture
active imagination	color schemes	designing	painting

Body/Kinesthetic: **Manipulating objects, Moving the body**
Include:

physical exercise	mime	folk dancing	role playing
body language	drama	physical gestures	charades

Musical/Rhythmic: **Tapping rhythms, Singing, Connecting with music**
Include:

musical performance	humming	musical composition	sounds
new words to songs	vibrations	rhythmic patterns	vocal tones

Interpersonal: **Working with partners or groups, Interacting**
Include:

giving feedback	group project	person to person communication
division of labor	collaborating	cooperative learning projects

Intrapersonal: **Working alone, Reflecting**
Include:

silent reflection	know thyself	guided imagery	journaling
emotional processing	metacognition	focusing skills	centering

POETRY FORMS

Cinquain

A cinquain poem is a five-line poem that does not rhyme. This poem describes a person, an idea, or a thing. Cinquain poems follow a special pattern:

Line 1—one word—noun
Line 2—two words—describes noun
Line 3—three words—action words—verb phrase
Line 4—four words—feelings about the noun
Line 5—one word—synonym for first word

God
Creative, Infinite
Loving, forgiving, leading
Great is your name
Creator

Haiku

This Japanese poetry form consists of three lines. The first and third lines have five syllables; the second line contains seven syllables. This form of poetry usually (but not always) deals with nature.

God's brush streaks the sky

Bursting with pinks and purples

A new day. Thank You!

VENN DIAGRAM

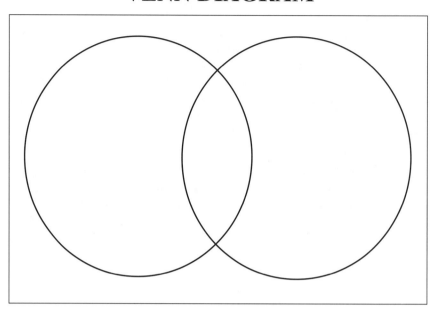

VENN DIAGRAM (Example)

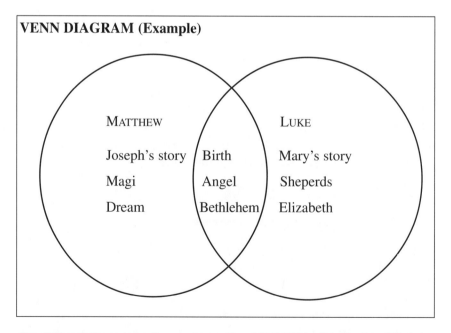

MATTHEW   LUKE

Joseph's story   Birth   Mary's story

Magi   Angel   Sheperds

Dream   Bethlehem   Elizabeth

PERSONAL "I AM" STATEMENTS

Jesus was a powerful leader in part because he knew who he was and what he was about. To help define who you are in this time and place, complete the following "I am" statements for yourself:

I am _____

I am _____

I am _____

I am _____

I am _____

I am _____

I am _____

THE "I AM" STATEMENTS OF JESUS

In the Gospel of John, Jesus says,

"I am the bread of life" (6:35);

"I am the light of the world" (8:12);

"I am the gate" (10:9);

"I am the good shepherd" (10:11);

"I am the resurrection and the life" (11:25);

"I am the way, and the truth, and the life" (14:6);

"I am the true vine" (15:1).

CONCEPT MAP

A concert map is a visual representation of an idea and many ideas that surround and are connected to it. One idea may lead to another.

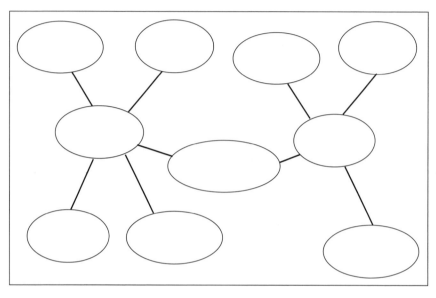

CONCEPT MAP (Example)

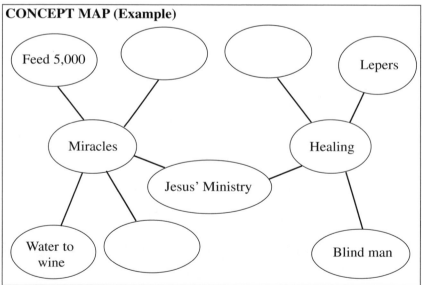

ANALOGY

An analogy is a figure of speech that connects things that may resemble other things with the words *like* or *as*. The kingdom parables are wonderful examples of analogy—"The kingdom of God is like . . ."

BREATH PRAYER

Select a five- to seven-word prayer addressing God and asking for what you need. (For example: "Gracious God, grant me your peace.") Take a deep, cleansing breath. As you breathe in, say the first few words ("Gracious God"); hold your breath for a few seconds. Then as you breathe out say the last few words ("grant me your peace"). Do this once or several times to calm yourself in the midst of traffic, in a check-out line, or any time you want to focus and connect with God. The beauty of this prayer is it is short and can be done anytime, anywhere.

PROBLEM SOLVING

This process, which varies slightly in different arenas, has several components. The main components of most problem-solving processes are:

Creative thinking	*Critical thinking*

Exploring the problem

talking about all areas of the problem	finding out what the real problem is

Gathering data

discovering all possible information	finding out what is critical data

Generating ideas

brainstorming many ideas to choose from	selecting the most workable ideas

Planning

discovering all possible strategies	making decisions about strategies that have the most possibilities

Finding Solutions

coming up with several possibilities for solving the problem	selecting the most workable one

Evaluation and feedback

checking out your solutions to make sure they work	making adjustments where needed

Each of these steps has a creative (lots of ideas—off-the-wall-thinking) and critical (looking at the ideas with discernment and critical judgment as to what will work best) thinking component to them. These activities use both hemispheres of the brain and produce insightful results in the thinking process. To be most successful both parts of each step are considered.

Bibliography

Armstrong, Thomas. *Multiple Intelligences in the Classroom*. Association for Supervision and Curriculum Development, 1999. ISBN: 0871202301.

Bruce, Barbara. *7 Ways of Teaching the Bible to Children*. Abingdon, 1996. ISBN: 0687020689.

_____. *Start Here: Teaching and Learning with Adults*. Discipleship Resources, 2000.

Gardner, Howard. *Frames of Mind: The Theory of Multiple Intelligences*. Basic Books, second anniv. edition, 1993. ISBN: 0465025102.

_____. *Intelligence Reframed: Multiple Intelligences for the 21st Century*. Basic Books, 1999. ISBN: 0465026109.

Goleman, Daniel. *Emotional Intelligence*. Bantam Books, 1996. ISBN: 055384007X.

Lazear, David G. *Seven Ways of Knowing: Teaching for Multiple Intelligences*. Skylight Publishing, second edition, 1991. ISBN: 0932935397.

_____. *Seven Ways of Teaching: The Artistry of Teaching for Multiple Intelligences*. Skylight Publishing, 1991. ISBN: 093293532X.

ANSWERS TO BIBLICAL BRAINBUSTER
(PAGE 89)

66 Books in the Bible

12 Tribes of Israel

40 Years Moses was Lost

12 Disciples of Jesus

10 Commandments God gave to Moses

16 Chapters in the Gospel of Mark

7 Days God Created the World

3 Days Jonah was in the Belly of a Fish

4 Horsemen of the Apocalypse

30 Pieces of Silver Judas was Paid